OTTERY ST M...

Cou...

Bransc...

SIDMOUTH

EXMOUTH

BUDLEIGH
SALTERTON

Sandy Bay

DAWLISH
Holcombe

TEIGNMOUTH

Shaldon

Maidencombe

Hope's Nose

Y

XHAM
Berry Head Country Park

Sands
bbacombe Head

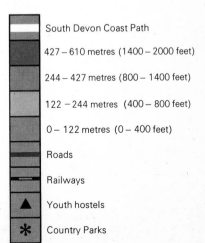

	South Devon Coast Path
	427 – 610 metres (1400 – 2000 feet)
	244 – 427 metres (800 – 1400 feet)
	122 – 244 metres (400 – 800 feet)
	0 – 122 metres (0 – 400 feet)
	Roads
	Railways
▲	Youth hostels
✳	Country Parks

South Devon Coast Path

Brian Le Messurier

Long-Distance Footpath Guide No. 9

London: Her Majesty's Stationery Office 1980

Published for the Countryside Commission

Cover:
An imaginary Devon setting by the artist, Vana Haggerty.

Pages x-xi View from Start Point looking towards Hallsands.

The maps in this guide are extracts from Ordnance Survey 1:50,000 maps (about 1¼in. to the mile), and have been prepared from O.S. sheets 192, 193, 201, 202.

Available through most booksellers is the Ordnance Survey Outdoor Leisure Man of South Devon, price £2.15. It covers the coast path at a scale of 1:25,000 (about 2½ in. to the mile), from Steeple Cove, near Bolt Head, eastwards to Goodrington Sands, Torbay. The Path is indicated by a thick, green, pecked line.

Drawings:
Vana Haggerty:

Photographs:
Roy J Westlake, ARPS

Long-distance footpath guides published for the Countryside Commission by HMSO:

The Pennine Way, by Tom Stephenson: 120 pages, £2·95 net
The Cleveland Way, by Alan Falconer: 144 pages, £2·95 net
The Pembrokeshire Coast Path, by John H Barrett:
124 pages, £2·95 net
Offa's Dyke Path, by John B Jones: 124 pages, £2·95 net
The Ridgeway Path, by Seán Jennett: 124 pages, £2·95 net
Cornwall Coast Path, by Edward C Pyatt: 112 pages, £2·50 net
South Downs Way, by Seán Jennett: 112 pages, £2·95 net
Dorset Coast Path, by Brian Jackman: 112 pages, £2·95 net

In preparation:
Somerset and North Devon Coast Path

Government Bookshops:
49 High Holborn, London W1CV 6HB
13a Castle Street, Edinburgh EH2 3AR
41 The Hayes, Cardiff CF1 1JW
Brazennose Street, Manchester M60 8AS
Southey House, Wine Street, Bristol BS1 2BQ
258 Broad Street, Birmingham B1 2HE
80 Chichester Street, Belfast BT1 4JY
Government publications are also available through booksellers

Prepared for the Countryside Commission by the Central Office of Information 1980.
Countryside Commission, John Dower House, Crescent Place, Cheltenham, Glos. GL50 3RA.

The waymark sign is used in plaque or stencil form by the Countryside Commission on long-distance footpaths

Printed in England for Her Majesty's Stationery Office by Balding & Mansell, Wisbech, Cambs.
ISBN 0 11 700896 6   Dd 596283   K 240

Contents

Maps of route

Maps reference

ROADS AND PATHS

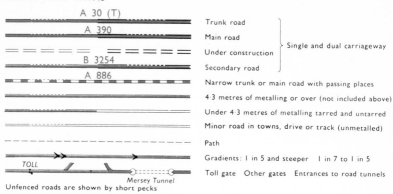

Trunk road
Main road
Under construction
Secondary road

} Single and dual carriageway

Narrow trunk or main road with passing places

4·3 metres of metalling or over (not included above)

Under 4·3 metres of metalling tarred and untarred

Minor road in towns, drive or track (unmetalled)

Path

Gradients: 1 in 5 and steeper   1 in 7 to 1 in 5

Toll gate   Other gates   Entrances to road tunnels

Mersey Tunnel

Unfenced roads are shown by short pecks

PUBLIC RIGHTS OF WAY

} Public paths { Footpath / Bridleway

Road used as a public path

Public rights of way indicated by these symbols have been derived from Definitive Maps as amended by later enactments or instruments held by Ordnance Survey on 1st February 1973 and are shown subject to the limitations imposed by the scale of mapping

The representation on this map of any other road, track or path is no evidence of the existence of a right of way

RAILWAYS

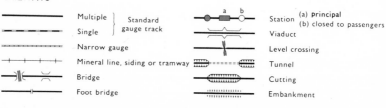

Multiple } Standard / Single } gauge track

Narrow gauge

Mineral line, siding or tramway

Bridge

Foot bridge

Station (a) principal (b) closed to passengers

Viaduct

Level crossing

Tunnel

Cutting

Embankment

WATER FEATURES

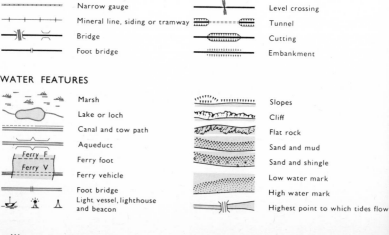

Marsh

Lake or loch

Canal and tow path

Aqueduct

Ferry foot

Ferry vehicle

Foot bridge

Light vessel, lighthouse and beacon

Slopes

Cliff

Flat rock

Sand and mud

Sand and shingle

Low water mark

High water mark

Highest point to which tides flow

GENERAL FEATURES

Electricity transmission line
(with pylons spaced conventionally)

Pipe line
(arrow indicates direction of flow)

Quarry

Open pit

Park or ornamental grounds

Bracken, heath and rough grassland

Dunes

↑ Broadcasting station (mast or tower)

⬯ Bus or coach station

▮ Church { with tower

▮ or { with spire

+ Chapel { without tower or spire

△ Triangulation pillar

⚙ Windmill (in use)

⚲ Windmill (disused)

⊺ Wind pump

▲ Youth hostel

RELIEF

Contour values are given to the nearest metre. The vertical interval is, however, 50 feet

Heights are to the nearest metre above mean sea level. Heights shown close to a triangulation pillar refer to the station height at ground level and not necessarily to the summit. Details of the summit height may be obtained from the Ordnance Survey

1 metre = 3·2808 feet   15·24 metres = 50 feet

———— 76 ————

·144

BOUNDARIES

— + — + — +   National

+ · + · + · +   District

— · — · — · —   County, Region or Islands Area

·················   Civil Parish or equivalent

NT   } National Trust { always open

nt   } National Trust { opening restricted

ABBREVIATIONS

P   Post office

PH   Public house

CH   Club house

·MP   Mile post

·MS   Mile stone

TH   Town hall, Guildhall or equivalent

PC   Public convenience (in rural areas)

·T ⎫
·A ⎬ Telephone call box ⎰ PO
·R ⎭   ⎱ AA
                          ⎰ RAC

ANTIQUITIES

VILLA   Roman

𝕿umulus   Non-Roman

+   Site of antiquity

⚔ 1066   Battlefield (with date)

TOURIST INFORMATION

ℹ   Information centre

South Devon Coast Path ———

Ⓜ   Country park

Proposed path   ················

Temporary route   — — — — — —

Having lived in the Devonshire countryside for a number of years, I thought I knew the South Devon coast reasonably well. How wrong I was! It wasn't until I came to write this guide and, therefore, walk this coast path that I realised there was so much to see and understand across so many planes of knowledge – geology, fauna, flora, beach life, history, and present day activity, each subject unusually varied within itself.

I am no stranger to coastal paths, for a great deal of my youth was spent walking those of Guernsey and of Sark. And the coastal area of south-west England is in the family blood. Both my mother and grandfather were born at St Anthony Head, beside the Cornwall Coast Path.

This is a magnificent path to walk, but a word of warning to those of you less than agile that parts of it are narrow and rugged, and the going is hard. Elsewhere the walking is easy and gentle – perfect for those times when strenuous exercise is not called for.

I hope that within the following pages I have conveyed some of the range of interest and scenic beauty to be found along the way. And maybe I shall have prompted the uncommitted to 'have a go' themselves!

My thanks are due to Bill Best Harris and Chris Blount of BBC Morning Sou' West, for permission to play back some of their tapes recorded on the path; to Ron Smith of Devon County Council; to Philip Carter of the South West Way Association; and to the staff of Slapton Ley Field Centre for assistance in matters of detail. The leaflets produced by the Centre I found most useful.

BLeM

On the Path, near Blackstone Point

A dramatic piece of coastline near Butter Cove, Bantham

Introduction

The South Devon Coast Path can best be summed up by one word: 'variety'. And for you, the traveller of this path, there should be at least one thing of interest from the mixture of towering cliffs, remote bays, popular holiday resorts, wildlife, wild flowers in abundance, the ruins of long-disused structures.

There are those stretches of this path where it is possible to walk for an hour or so without seeing anyone, along others there always seems to be someone around, particularly on headlands such as Berry Head. In many places the land surface is so smooth and flat you can imagine you are out for a gentle stroll; elsewhere you are faced with a succession of switchback hills that make the pulse race and the rucksack seem to double in weight.

Providing enjoyable breaks are the six ferry crossings to be made across six estuaries. And at the Erme estuary, where there is no ferry, the only way to get to the other side is by wading across.

There is variation in the rocks along the way, making the scenery change from mile to mile, and this is reflected in the flora. There is no monotony on this coast path.

A chain of fast-growing holiday towns from Brixham to Exmouth has meant a discontinuity of natural landscape on the central section. But this should not deter you from walking from Torquay to Shaldon, which is one of the most interesting lengths of the whole path and, towards the north end, very strenuous.

The coastal stretches from Bovisand Bay to Berry Head and from Orcombe Point (Exmouth) to Lyme Regis (except Seaton) are designated as areas of outstanding natural beauty. Three lengths have also been defined as heritage coasts – areas of high-quality coastal scenery deserving special measures to conserve their character. They are the stretches from Bolt Tail to Start Point; the still-forbidden coast between Kingswear Castle and Man Sands; and the East Devon cliffs from Sidmouth into Dorset.

If still further proof of the worth of this coast path is required one need only add that considerable mileages are under the protection of the National Trust and various other bodies concerned with the conservation of wildlife and flora.

In a later chapter the origin of the coastguard track round the cliffs is described. This was mooted by W. Harding Thompson in his 1932 survey of rural Devon as a route which should be dedicated to public use and maintained by the local authorities. This was probably the first suggestion of a coastal footpath round the coast of Devon, but nothing came of it.

However, in the late 1940s, with a different public attitude to access to the countryside, two official reports, the Dower report and the Hobhouse report, recommended specific coastal paths, including those of Devon. The 1949 National Parks and Access to the Countryside Act confirmed the proposal and negotiations began at local level for a path right round the coast from Minehead in Somerset to Poole in Dorset to be called the South-West Peninsula Coast Path. The South Devon section was approved in 1959, but not officially opened until 14 September 1974, when a joint ceremony to mark the inauguration of the Dorset and South Devon paths was held on Beer Head. The ceremony was performed by Lord Amory.

Estimates vary as to the length of the South Devon Coast Path. Officially it is 149 kilometres, but it really depends on whether you count those stretches which are not official parts of the path; for instance, through Salcombe and Brixham, which have to be walked to get to the other side. My own appraisal makes it 179 kilometres.

Advice on the logistics of tackling the path is contained in the chapter Planning the walk, but I would just say here, the path is there to be enjoyed; to walk it thinking only of the destination is to miss the point.

The natural scene

Every living thing on the coast, whether it be plant or animal, depends for its existence on the rocks and the soil and their disposition in relation to water and sea. Given that the rocks along the South Devon Coast Path have an abundant diversity, it follows that the theme of variety I touched upon in the introductory chapter will show itself in the range of habitats in the natural arena.

Because of the multitude of possibilities it is impossible in this chapter to indicate many separate species, so the space is better used to indicate where the various habitats may be found.

Sea coasts suggest cliffs, and cliffs automatically make one think of sea birds. Their main requirements are high, inaccessible cliffs on a thrusting promontory or island adjacent to a good feeding area, and because most bird activity takes place at breeding time the fruitful months for observation are April, May and June. Wembury Point looks across to the Great Mew Stone, a favourite breeding station, while other sites going eastwards are Stoke Point, Burgh Island, the coast from Bolt Tail to Start Point, Scabbacombe Head (not on the path), Berry Head, Hope's Nose, Brandy Head, Ladram Bay and Beer Head. Gannets 'dive-bombing' for fish can sometimes be seen off the coast, and the free-soaring fulmar is extending its range, but it is the cry of the ubiquitous herring gull which gets into one's head. At Brixham their numbers have grown to such an extent that they are now, unfortunately, regarded as pests.

A good place to observe wading birds is where the rivers meet the sea and tidal estuaries uncover the mud-flats twice daily. The dunlin is the most common wader, sometimes being seen in flocks several thousand strong. Curlews with their haunting cry are often heard and seen, as are redshanks, lapwings and the smartly-plumaged oystercatcher. The avocet, a black and white bird with a long upturned bill, winters on several of the larger south coast estuaries. The river-mouth sites on the coast path are the Yealm, Erme, Avon, Teign, Exe, Otter and Axe.

The well-named turnstone may be seen at Wembury Point and the Exe estuary throughout the year, though in fewer numbers in the summer. At this time of year it

TAVISTOCK

NEWTON ABBOT

TOTNES

PLYMOUTH

DARTMOUTH

KINGSBRIDGE

SALCOMBE

0   10 Miles

0   15 Kilometres

4

AXMINSTER

OTTERY ST MARY

XETER

LYME REGIS

SEATON

SIDMOUTH

EXMOUTH

BUDLEIGH
SALTERTON

DAWLISH

TEIGNMOUTH

BAY

XHAM

South Devon Coast Path

Oligocene

Eocene

Cretaceous

Jurassic

New Red Sandstone

Carboniferous

Devonian

Extrusive

Intrusive

Metamorphic

5

possesses a very eye-catching face pattern. The coast at Wembury is a bird sanctuary, and 32 hectares of the estuary side of Dawlish Warren is a nature reserve. This is the only known British mainland site of the sand crocus, and the tree lupin also grows here.

You don't expect to find a conifer woodland on a coast path, but there is a small softwood plantation on the top of High Peak, west of Sidmouth. It is unfortunate that the trees smother the summit, but this afforestation has encouraged the siskin to make its home here. About 10 hectares of cliff to the east of Sidmouth are protected as nature reserves. These sloping cliffs offer a secure foothold for blackthorn and bramble to establish themselves, and the usual thicket birds – wrens, yellowhammers, stone-chats, and whitethroats – have colonised the shelter so formed.

South Devon is not renowned for its sand dunes, but they can be seen at Bantham and Dawlish Warren. Large numbers of, mainly, summer visitors are attracted to the areas where sand dunes form, so, naturally, they are at risk from trampling, particularly by children's feet. Constant pressure from feet destroys the marram (shore grass) which binds the sand, resulting in a gully forming through

Tranquil sailing scene at Salcombe

the centre of the dune. In time, the force of the wind under-
cuts the stable chines on either side forcing them to
collapse into the gully. What is known as a 'blow-out' has
occurred and the damage can only be remedied by repair
work with brushwood and the dune fenced off. It is
sufficient to say that there were 375,100 day visitors to
Dawlish Warren during the five months from May to
September!

Slapton Ley is the largest natural freshwater lake in
Devon, and extends to 97 hectares. An account of this is
given as it arises in the path description chapters. So, too,
is the East Devon landslip area.

I indicated earlier that a variety of rocks begets a
diversity of flora, and this is evident on the limestone cliffs
which flank Torbay. Certain plants are lime-tolerant, so
you can expect to see a flora on, say, Berry Head, that is
not found elsewhere. It really is worth getting the Berry
Head nature trail guide, which is on sale at the car park
entrance. Wembury has its own nature trail guide.
Slapton Ley and Slapton Sands also have their own, published by Slapton Ley Field Centre. In East Devon the
Devon Trust for Nature Conservation has issued a nature
trail guide for Salcombe Hill, Sidmouth, which can be

bought in local shops.

The many different kinds of rocks along the coast are noticed as you come to them, but it is worth reflecting on their wealth of colour when looking at the coast as a whole. There is greensand, chalk, red sandstone, limestone (both grey and red, as at Petit Tor), and the grey slate and schistose rocks of the South Hams, much of it encrusted with hoary, salt-tolerant lichens which bestow a yellow or green tincture when seen close up.

If you are on the look-out for wildlife you need to be constantly alert. And when you see *any* creature, approach it without too much disturbance if you want to observe it going about its ordinary business. Rabbits are fairly common, and I have seen grey squirrels in the Landslip. Seals and porpoises are sometimes to be seen in the sea. At Hoist Point, between Wonwell and Challaborough, I saw a badger – normally a nocturnal animal – come out of a clump of brambles and waddle along the path for about 25 metres before diving into another bush on the opposite side; and this at five o'clock on a July afternoon!

It is a mistake to think that interesting living things can only be seen in nature reserves. The multitude of butterflies that seem to be feeding on every summer flower along those parts of the path beside agricultural land or golf courses, are evidence of natural fecundity which knows no designation of reserves or sanctuaries.

The imprint of man on the coast

The South Devon coast is not renowned for an abundance of visible antiquities. In that respect Cornwall is indisputably the richer county.

There are the remains of a few Iron Age forts dating from about AD 200. Bolt Tail (the best preserved beside the path), Berry Head (destroyed), High Peak and Berry Cliff Camp. These were places to retreat to in times of inter-tribal warfare.

Moving along the path you notice many place names incorporating the word 'warren', and there are many more to be found on the 2½-inch map. They used to be places where rabbits were encouraged to breed freely and then culled for their flesh and fur. In the days before refrigeration the meat of the rabbit was highly prized to eke out the otherwise meatless days of winter.

Yet another common place name embodies the word 'beacon'. This refers to the practice of lighting warning fires on prominent coastal features to warn of possible invasion.

While on your way you will come across groups of coastguard cottages – many of them are mentioned in the path description chapters. Few are still in use as homes for coastguards and their families, although those at Noss Mayo and Beer are just that. Most have been converted for summer holiday use, and one terrace, east of Salcombe, has become the Gara Rock Hotel. They are quite distinctive and easily identified as to what they originally were. Built in the last century to house the men recruited to stamp out smuggling, they are situated in out-of-the-way places – Mothecombe and Man Sands for instance.

The illicit import of valuable commodities into this country, thus evading the payment of duty, had become a lucrative business for large numbers of people. So in January 1822 the 'Coast Guard' was formed to counter this trade and look-outs were built on certain headlands. It could be said that the existence of this coast path is due to the daily passage of patrolling coastguards, for they performed this role until 1913 although the battle to beat the smugglers had been won back in 1840.

The role of HM Coastguard today is a very different one. Equipped with modern communications techniques, it is responsible for the co-ordination of search and rescue around the miles of coastline and is completely dedicated to the guarding and saving of life at sea.

Many headlands still have coastguard look-outs – small huts with panoramic windows on all sea-facing sides – but Berry Head is the one that attracts attention through being manned at all times. Others only come into service when the weather turns particularly sour and then part-timers, or Auxiliaries as they are called, come on duty.

Another aspect of saving life at sea are the disused lifeboat houses to be seen at Inner Hope, Salcombe, Teignmouth and Exmouth. The South Devon lifeboats are now kept permanently moored in deep water.

Up to about sixty years ago a busy trade in a variety of cargoes was carried on round the South Devon coast. Ships took Berry Head and Walls Hill limestone to numerous destinations, both for building purposes and for burning.

Boats moored in the Barbican, Plymouth

Dawlish: its sea wall railway was engineered by Brunel

Every inlet had its own limekiln where limestone was burnt to produce lime to spread on the land. Coal was used in the firing, so this material had also to be brought by sea to the site and laboriously unloaded onto the beaches. If you are at all imaginative, it is possible to picture small ketches high and dry between tides at out-of-the-way places like Wonwell, Bantham, Man Sands and Cock-wood. Bantham was also what would now be called a trans-shipment port. Here, cargoes were transferred to barges which took them four or five kilometres up the Avon to Aveton Gifford. Unloading and loading was thirsty work, so there were two pubs in this tiny place to provide refreshment, and they are still there today. The coastal trade wasn't solely commercial. A hundred years ago a weekly 'market packet' took people from Kings-bridge to Plymouth, calling at Salcombe on the way.

A great deal of Devon's best agricultural land is visible from the coast path – grades 1 and 2 in the official Ministry of Agriculture classification. The good soil meets the sea-board for most of the way, except in East Devon, where the infertile greensand plateaux remain uncultivated. It is a matter of considerable regret that the built-up hinterland of the Torbay urban sprawl is almost entirely on the most productive land in the county.

Sheep are the animals most commonly seen from the path. They could be any of numerous different breeds as no one type is predominant and they are often crossed. In places they graze on the open cliffs, especially where they slope gently to the rocks. Between Gara Point and Stoke Point is such a stretch.

Traditional cattle of the area are the South Devon breed, whose colour range is from pale yellow to reddish brown. It is the largest bovine in the country, and is an ideal dual-purpose animal, providing rich milk and sturdy bullocks. However, in under thirty years their numbers in the South Hams have dropped from about 12,000 to more like 2,000, while during the same period the Friesian has increased vastly in numbers. But new strains are being tried all the time, and Charolais crossed with Galloway or Welsh Black cattle are often seen.

The rough grazing of cliff land might be thought suitable for goats, but I have only seen them on Bolt Head where they sometimes get into precarious situations.

A whole range of crops can be seen from the path – cereals, roots, grass and brassicas – their colours changing with the seasons.

The impact of man on the coast would not be complete without a mention of the holiday industry, and this is covered in the next chapter.

Brunel's 'atmospheric' railway the pumping house at Starcross

The growth of the South Devon holiday industry

So much of the South Devon coast is taken up with seaside resorts that it may be of interest to give a short outline explaining how the holiday industry came to have such a firm footing.

To understand why people first started visiting the coast for pleasure it is necessary to go back to the seventeenth and eighteenth centuries, and the fashion of taking the waters at inland spas.

Bath and Buxton had achieved some fame as curative centres as early as the 1570s, but at that time no provision was made for pleasure and entertainment. The use of mineral waters in the therapeutic process was something the Romans had understood, and throughout the Middle Ages the ruins of Roman Bath had never been quite deserted.

The revival of the custom was due to the Renaissance, and reflected a similar trend on the Continent. The name 'spa' is taken from a watering-place in the province of Liége, Belgium.

Gradually the spas began to provide diversions for their patients, and as a result people started visiting them as much for the entertainment they provided as for the cures they boasted of. At this point they became fashionable.

In the eighteenth century various physicians began to encourage sea bathing, and even the drinking of salt water, and this was a movement which went on throughout the century. Probably the most influential publication was Dr Richard Russell's *Dissertation on the Use of Sea-Water in the Diseases of the Glands*, which went into several editions in the 1750s. It was reasoned that sea water was simply a mineral water of the kind sought at spas.

Scarborough, being an established spa on the coast, was well situated to take advantage of the new fashion, while in the south the fishing village of Brighthelmstone (now Brighton) became London's premier contact with the sea.

Aerial view of Exmouth (*Aerofilms Ltd*)

Naturally, the inland spas suffered. The sea was there for the taking, while mineral springs were in short supply.

The first of the Devon seaside resorts to become well known was Exmouth during the first half of the eighteenth century, and this was because of its proximity to Exeter which at that time was a provincial centre of considerable importance. Little seems to have been provided in the way of entertainment until the Assembly Rooms – a spa word – were opened in 1817. Here the elite met for cards, dancing and other social gatherings. In 1792 the attractive houses on the Beacon had been built, and among the long-term residents were Lady Nelson and Lady Byron. An account written in 1842 mentions 'several billiard and reading rooms', and there were bathing machines on the beach and 'excellent warm sea-water baths'.

Teignmouth, situated in a similar estuary-mouth, was quick to follow Exmouth, and soon became fashionable. Keats and Fanny Burney stayed here, and the large classical Assembly Rooms of 1826 are still in the entertainment business. The town had been destroyed by a French bombardment in 1690, and the replacement buildings, much sprucer than the average fishermen's dwellings in other seaports, provided comfortable accommodation for the visitors.

Dawlish was described by the traveller/writer W G Maton (1794) as 'a neat, new village, not frequented by summer visitors until within the last two or three years'. At all events it had a Bath House in 1805 and a suite of Public Rooms in 1812.

Sidmouth had received a visit from the King of England in 1791 and this gave the tiny fishing village the respectability of Court patronage. This visit was followed by a lengthy stay during the winter of 1819–20 by the Duke and Duchess of Kent with their infant daughter Victoria. Maton, in a 1794 view of Sidmouth, wrote: 'It is much frequented in the bathing season, and many families continue their residence even during the winter. The situation is certainly a very delightful one'.

The story of Torquay is more complicated and bedevilled by a kind of folklore which has attributed the development of the town to the presence in Torbay of the Channel Fleet during the Napoleonic Wars. The officers are supposed to have lodged their families in the embryo resort.

However, Percy Russell, in his deeply-researched book *A History of Torquay and the Famous Anchorage of Torbay* found no evidence for this theory. He was firmly of the view that the medical officers on duty with the Fleet understood the climatic benefits of the sheltered site of Torquay and recommended it to consumptive patients. And certainly, while historians may disagree as to the cause of Torquay's rise to seaside eminence, there is no argument that it was as a haven for invalids that the town increased its reputation.

Teignmouth-Shaldon ferry about to beach at Shaldon

View from Langstone Rock, looking towards Dawlish Warren

View from Peak Hill looking towards Sidr

Dr A B Granville, the author of *The Spas of England and Principal Sea-Bathing Places* (1841) found in Torquay that every bedroom was furnished with a 'spitting pot'. We know too that Elizabeth Barrett Browning spent three years in Torquay suffering from consumption.

The development of a seaside watering place two hundred years ago depended on several factors. An attractive site with a modicum of accommodation was needed as a starter, and to this had to be added a medical recommendation. A great fillip accrued if Royalty happened to stay, but local enterprise in the form of the sale of plots for the building of the better type of house and the provision of some form of public meeting place was needed to confirm the resort's standing. The final factor was when the Napoleonic wars closed the Continent to English travellers.

Those who were denied the gratification of foreign travel were recommended to try Torquay, where a mild climate prevailed, and where even the newly-provided villas were being given Italian-sounding names like Villa Borghese and Villa Como, and what is more, they were built in an Italian style. Ruskin christened it 'The Italy of England'.

The entrepreneurial landowner behind this sharp piece of showmanship was Sir Lawrence Palk, and the Cary family was also involved. Palk had been on the Grand Tour, and had absorbed the flavour of the Mediterranean coastline. He and other 'Grand Tourists' saw similarities in the conjunction of sea and land in Torbay with the Riviera and the Bay of Naples.

In 1833 Princess Victoria visited Torquay with her mother. With this Royal favour all the criteria for the establishment of Torquay as a successful resort were now complete.

But there remained one bonus. The railway arrived (at what is now Torre station) in 1848, and from that time the population gained rapidly; in the thirty years after 1841, the population increased from 5,982 to 21,657. The improvement of the county's roads in the early years of the century had helped communications but did not achieve the transport revolution the railways accomplished.

What of Paignton during these years? Back at the beginning of the century it had been twice the size of Torquay – 1,575 people, as against 838 in 1801 – but the inhabitants had been grouped in the old village a short distance inland. The qualities which endowed Torquay with a special character for many made it unattractive to others, so that Paignton was complementary to its upstart neighbour. The hills of Torquay were the foil for the flatter topography of Paignton, which had better beaches than Torquay. If Torquay catered originally for the patricians, Paignton was glad to have the plebs.

The railway was a long time pushing on further, and didn't reach Paignton until eleven years after it had reached Torquay, on the way opening a new station to serve Torquay.

All this time the East Devon resorts were without rail connections, though Exmouth tried to capitalise on the fact that Brunel's railway passed along the other side of the estuary, but crossing the wide and often choppy channel by rowing boat didn't encourage those who could

Torquay harb

go straight to a seaside destination without such hardships. Exmouth eventually got its branch line rail link with Exeter in 1861.

The other East Devon resorts, Seaton, Sidmouth and Budleigh Salterton were joined up to the London and South Western Railway in 1868, 1874 and 1897 respectively. The tardy arrival of the railway in these towns does not seem to have concerned them. It must have been plain by now that they lacked that vital natural element so necessary for the success of the family holiday – sand.

As the nineteenth century wore on the emphasis changed from sea water to sea air. Climate became more important and beaches were necessary for children's enjoyment. The weekly half-day holiday granted in the middle of the century was followed by the Bank Holiday Act of 1891, and later, holidays with pay. The seaside holiday pattern was established.

From the 1950s onwards, other forces have been at work to alter what was sometimes referred to as the traditional English holiday. Widespread car ownership has given the public a taste of the pleasures of mobility and independence, so that many of the small guest houses and private hotels which thrived in the heyday of the railway era have been converted to holiday flats.

Walking the South Devon Coast Path you will notice the self-catering fashion in the rash of chalet, caravan and camping sites. A number of these are mentioned in the

atcher Rock,
Hope's Nose,
Torquay

path description chapters, but Brixham seems to have more than its share of chalet sites, while Sandy Bay, on the eastern outskirts of Exmouth, must have the largest caravan site in South Devon.

Brixham developed late as a holiday resort, being a place to visit from Torquay or Paignton until the post-war years. But as available land for development got used up elsewhere in the Torbay area, the Brixham hinterland succumbed to the pressure. Holiday camps are another post-war element in the leisure scene, but they don't impinge much on the views along the path, except at Seaton.

At the up-market end of the holiday spectrum most of the changes in the last thirty years have centred on the popularity of sailing, and the suitability of the coastline from Plymouth to Exmouth for this activity. East of Exmouth the scarcity of harbours and inlets has limited any developments. Marinas, crowded moorings, dinghy parks, yachting boutiques, boatels and the adaptation of certain hotels at Salcombe and Dartmouth to the needs of the sailing fraternity will all be noticed as you pass on your way.

One final change needs to be remarked upon. South Devon is a favourite place for second homes, so the winter walker must not be surprised to find many of the more attractive cottages shuttered and wearing an unlived-in look. They may only be used for a few weeks in each year.

Progressing round the coast I found that it was the scars of holiday and post-war residential growth that jarred on my senses. The early developers, unhampered by planning regulations, nevertheless had an understanding of the fitness and scale of their buildings. We must hope that no further permanently-damaging encroachments into coastal areas by the gimcrackery of short-term exploitation will be allowed.

Planning the walk

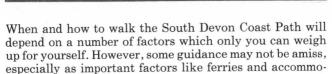

When and how to walk the South Devon Coast Path will depend on a number of factors which only you can weigh up for yourself. However, some guidance may not be amiss, especially as important factors like ferries and accommodation will affect the pre-walk planning.

Surely no other stretch of a long-distance path has its continuity broken so often by water. But if this is taken into account in your planning, no inconvenience should be felt. Indeed the ferry crossings and the ford at Erme Mouth provide pleasant interludes during progress round the coast.

First of all it must be understood that there are six ferries to take and one ford to cross between Plymouth and Exmouth. Of the ferries, three run only in the summer and one of these operates only for one hour in the morning and one hour in the afternoon (see Ferries and river crossings, p. 106). The ford can only be used for one hour either side of low water, and the alternative road route round the estuary is many kilometres long.

So this is not a walk for the off-season. That much must be admitted. (From Exmouth to Lyme Regis there are no ferries, so this bit makes a pleasant three-day stint at any time of year). You must plan your progress having regard to these limitations, and having read the chapter on Ferries and river crossings, otherwise you could arrive at, say, Mothecombe, late one afternoon with the tide rising and no possibility of fording the estuary until the following day.

Bus services are also more infrequent in off-season months, and refreshment points are often closed. Where 'refreshments' are indicated in the path description chapters this usually means in 'the season' only. However, the path passes through many towns where buses and refreshments are available all year round.

Accommodation is another important element to consider at the planning stage. The initial question to ask is: am I camping or spending the nights under someone's roof? Whatever is decided upon some preparation is necessary. Here the advice must be to get good up-to-date local information and book in advance. It really is not sensible to arrive at a seaside village in a peak holiday period with the evening well advanced expecting to find a room. Even camp sites near the coast get full, but a farmer may be willing to allow a small lightweight tent in the corner of a field so long as he is asked first. To find out what accommodation is available in a given area, write to the tourist information centre nearest to your route. All the towns listed in the Gazetteer section have information centres, except Beer, but many of them are seasonal. Always enclose a large, stamped addressed envelope when writing, and if you have any difficulty, write to the West Country Tourist Board. (Addresses of all organisations mentioned in this chapter are given under Useful addresses on p 104.)

The South West Way Association issues an annual guide to the whole of the South-West Peninsula Coast Path, which includes accommodation addresses, and the Ramblers' Association publishes an annual *Bed, Breakfast and Bus Guide*. There are YHA youth hostels at Plymouth, Bigbury-on-Sea, Salcombe, Strete, Maypool (up-river from Dartmouth, east bank), Exeter and Beer.

Probably the most comprehensive information on camping is contained in the Devon Tourism Office's *Guide to Farmhouse Accommodation and Touring Caravan/Camping Sites*, but there are commercial camping guides for sale on bookstalls.

All bus and ferry services in the county are listed in the annual Devon timetable of the Western National Bus Company. It also includes useful facts like the phone numbers and exact addresses of tourist information centres, the population, early closing days of the main towns, the location of hospitals, and the main rail and express coach services linking the west country. Unfortunately it weighs ¾lb, but if you wish to eliminate any surplus weight you can tear out the pages you won't need. It is certainly essential to have a copy by you at the planning stage. This indispensible handbook comes out annually in May.

What you carry with you will depend on the type of overnight stops you intend to make. Obviously, if you are a lightweight camper you will be self-sufficient, although you will have to top yourself up with food and fuel at the towns en route. There is a scarcity of ordinary supply stores until Bigbury-on-Sea is reached, assuming one has set out from Plymouth.

One of the joys of the route is coming across a delightful cove which tempts you down for a swim. The advice is, therefore, to carry a towel and bathing gear near the top of your kit. After a swim the wet things can be tied to the outside of the rucksack to dry. A camera and binoculars are worth carrying too.

There are some very rough and steep stretches, particularly west of Bigbury-on-Sea, between Maidencombe and Labrador Bay, and in the East Devon landslips, so my advice is to wear boots with moulded rubber soles. They give the support and the security that shoes never can.

The same lengths of path can be uncomfortable for those clad in shorts, so trousers are recommended on the less-used sections. It shouldn't be necessary to add that some form of waterproof garment is essential as well as a warm jumper to ward off those chilly sea breezes.

However, I shouldn't want to deter people who may just be out for a stroll on the path and dressed in ordinary casual clothes. There are plenty of undemanding sections which can be walked without looking like a mountaineer: Plymouth to Wembury, Noss Mayo to Revelstoke church, Bantham to Hope Cove, the National Trust land accessible from Bolberry Down, Hallsands to Torcross, Berry Head, Torquay to Babbacombe, Teignmouth to Dawlish Warren, Exmouth to Sandy Bay, Beer to Beer Head or Seaton, and Seaton to the western end of the Landslip National Nature Reserve.

Plymouth to Thurlestone

(37 kilometres)

Look at a map of Plymouth, the Sound and its surroundings, and given that Cremyll is the obvious place for the Cornwall Coast Path to end (or start), then Turnchapel is the incontestable jumping-off place for the South Devon Coast Path. This small village on the south side of the Cattewater is the topographical twin to Cremyll across the Sound, but alas, it has no ferry linking it to Plymouth. The ferry was discontinued many years ago, but is still shown on some maps, including the current 2½-inch map. (For Plymouth, see Gazetteer chapter.) Despite this deficiency Turnchapel can be reached from Plymouth bus station by a fairly frequent number 7 bus which has its terminus 300 metres up the hill from Turnchapel waterfront at RAF Mountbatten guardroom. The pedantic walker will nevertheless want to get down to sea level to say that he has started from the point of origin of the path. Turnchapel is a pleasant backwater, with a few narrow streets and an emphasis on marine repairs, but there is little of interest to make you want to linger. Retrace your steps up the steep hill, past the playing field to a T-junction where you turn right.

The massive walls facing you here belong to Stamford Fort, now a Holiday Centre and Country Club, but built only a little over a hundred years ago as one of a large number of forts and batteries to protect the Plymouth naval base from the threat of French sea power. The introduction of ironclad warships and more powerful guns had temporarily eroded Britain's naval superiority, so Plymouth, as well as Portsmouth, Chatham and Dover, was given this expensive defence system. Since Lord Palmerston was the man who created the Royal Commission in 1859 'to consider the Defences of the United Kingdom' the forts which resulted became known as Palmerston forts and latterly Palmerston follies. But as he died in 1865, before many of them were built, he can hardly be blamed for the enormous expenditure of public money. Not only were the seaward approaches to Plymouth

Mew Stone,
red from
ury beach

25

Bovisand be
and Fort Bo

defended, but the hinterland was also protected by a
crescent of ten forts and batteries stretching from the
Plym to the Tamar. When Stamford Fort was being built
it was discovered that there was dead ground in Jennycliff
Bay which the guns could not reach, so the hill in front
was pared down. In doing this a Romano-British cemetery
was discovered. Then in about 1918, when the RAF station
at Mountbatten was being built, many more finds were
uncovered, some of them putting the date of the settlement
at 1000 BC, and suggesting a continuous occupation to
late Roman times.

Leaving Stamford Fort behind, you soon come to the
pleasant open slopes above Jennycliff Bay (refreshments),
which can also be reached by open-top bus on summer
weekends from Plymouth bus station – service number 53.
The same bus goes on to Bovisand. Superb views across to
Mount Edgcumbe and the Maker peninsula now reveal
themselves. To the right (north-west) is the Plymouth
built-up area with the dockyard beyond up the Hamoaze.
The only island in Plymouth Sound is Drake's Island, now
an adventure training base. Sailing, canoeing, rowing,
climbing, are all practised from there. Straight ahead on
the skyline of Staddon Heights is an enormous blank wall.
This was the back or safety wall of a nineteenth century
rifle range. The route continues along what is virtually a
marine drive, and at weekends during the summer traffic
along it can be quite heavy. Where the road bears inland,
and just before a small combe is reached, a path goes off
to the right along the cliff. This is the South Devon
Coast Path.

As it opens out after an initial vegetated section the Breakwater comes in view. This massive defence against southerly gales was started in 1812, to a design of John Rennie, and not finished until 1848, by which time 3½ million tons of stone had been dumped along a marked line by barges bringing the material from Oreston quarries up the Cattewater.

At the foot of the cliff is Bovisand Harbour and Fort. The Harbour was constructed between 1816 and 1824 to enable ships to take on fresh water without having to go right into the dockyard. A reservoir was built up the valley behind Bovisand Bay and a pipe brought the water to the ships.

Fort Bovisand is one of the Palmerston forts, and is the best preserved of all the mid-nineteenth century Plymouth defences. It is now in use as a training base for underwater activities and as a marine study centre. Oil rig divers are trained there, and so too are members of HM Services. It is also used for training in such pastimes as canoeing, sailing and wind surfing.

The path continues, crossing an artificial ravine by way of a footbridge before meeting the road near some converted coastguard cottages. This ravine was originally cut to transport ammunition and supplies, by means of a form of cable-worked device, from the top of the hill to the Fort below.

Bovisand Bay (refreshments) is the first of many beaches on the South Devon Coast Path having a backdrop of caravans and chalets. Noticeable here is that the earlier haphazard growth of summer bungalows seems to fit into the landscape better than the regular rows of chalets which have been added more recently.

If you started from Turnchapel, you have now covered about 3 kilometres, and over that distance have passed across several different bands of rock. At Turnchapel you were on Plymouth limestone, moving on to tuffs at Jennycliff. Abreast of Staddon Heights there were grits and shales and at Bovisand, slate, but the low cliffs bear deposits of head. This is a conglomerate material brought down from levels further up. You will read about this kind of overlay further on. This rapid transition from one geological structure to another is characteristic of the South Devon coast.

The path follows the cliff edge to Heybrook Bay, a bit of suburbia-by-the-sea, passing the aptly named Shag Stone which may well be serving as a perch for shags or cormorants if the sea is not running too high. Beyond Heybrook Bay (service 61 to Plymouth) the path passes within metres of the guns of HMS Cambridge, a Royal Navy gunnery school. A sign warns: 'Gunfire noise. When red flag is flying please use alternative route through Ministry of Defence property'. (A similar warning notice is shown if you are approaching from the east.) The alternative route is signposted throughout the grounds of HMS Cambridge.

Advance notice a few days prior to firing can be obtained by contacting the Range Officer (Plymouth 53740, Ext. 412) during working hours, or the Quartermaster (Ext. 406) at any other time. Obviously, it is inadvisable to linger or picnic on the path in front of the guns.

The Great Mew Stone (one of three similarly named stones you pass before reaching Torbay) is now the major object in view, and the noise of its gull population is with you for the next kilometre or so. (The name Mew means gull.)

The side of this stone that you see from Wembury Point presents such a steep face that it is hard to believe that it ever supported human life. But as you move eastwards the remains of a dwelling can be clearly seen on the gentler-sloped south-facing side. In 1744 a local man was banished to the Great Mew Stone for seven years by the local magistrates, so he took his family. When he left, his daughter, Black Bess, decided to remain. Staying on the island, she married and had three children. In the 1800s, one Samuel Wakeham set up home there, created a garden and kept pigs and poultry. On behalf of the owner he acted as warrener, safe-guarding the rabbits out of season. Eventually he was caught smuggling and retired ashore as a boatman in Plymouth. The island is now owned by

Kestrel

View from the F
above Wembury b

28

the Ministry of Defence, but the Devon Trust for Nature Conservation has access rights. Fulmars, kittiwakes and other sea birds breed there and it has a large population of rats.

The path continues to follow the edge of low cliffs, but the gradual slope of the fields between Wembury Point and Wembury church, now visible, provide you with another example of head. The original cliff line is back from the beach, where the steeper slopes begin. Wembury beach has a rich inter-tidal variety of plants and animals, and because it is near Plymouth it has been over-used by educational parties. So the Wembury Amenity Society, with commendable enterprise, has produced its own illustrated nature trail guide covering the beach and cliffs. Conservation and identification, rather than collection, are stressed. The guide is obtainable at the National Trust Wembury Mill shop. Refreshments are also available here. (57 or 60 bus to Plymouth.) Wembury church should now be visited. Standing as it does in such a conspicuous position, away from the settlement it served, it is assumed that it was originally sited there to serve as a landmark for shipping. It has some notable monuments and good modern woodwork. John Galsworthy's ancestors came from Wembury and he made a pilgrimage here in 1912 – later transferring his own kinship to the Forsyte family. In his *Swan Song*, Soames Forsyte visited a similarly-sited fictional church stated to be in Dorset.

Newton Ferrers, viewed from Noss Mayo

Buzzard

For the next 2 kilometres the path is in National Trust land and takes you towards the beautiful wooded mouth of the Yealm estuary (pronounced Yam). The path passes Rocket House, where coastguard apparatus used to be stored, then drops steeply down to Warren Point where on the rocks the ferry can be hailed. From this spot you can go right to Noss Mayo and the coast path beyond, or left to Newton Ferrers and then a number 94 bus to Plymouth. (See Ferries chapter.)

On landing upon Noss Mayo shore, take a look at the restored ferryman's sign exhibited there. It says, *inter alia*: 'Ferriage for every person on weekdays 1d; the like on Sundays 2d. For every pony and ass 3d'.

At the top of the ferry steps, you turn right to go along a narrow footpath and on towards a wide drive. (If walking east to west, on nearing Noss Mayo turn down a path opposite steep steps in woods saying 'Private. To Coast Guard Station'.) This gently rising drive is the so-called Nine Mile Drive. It was cut by local fishermen, as an off-season job, towards the end of the last century at the behest of Lord Revelstoke. The drive encircled his estate which was based on Membland, and along it he would take his distinguished visitors to show off his property and the cliff scenery. It is a magnificent high-level walk, and continues for 8 kilometres without any serious ups and downs, which is what you'd expect of a route engineered for recreational horse-drawn transport.

You are now in the South Hams, that large chunk of Devon between Dartmoor and the sea, having the Yealm as its western boundary and the Dart marking its eastern limit – but there is no general agreement about exact

confines. The massive masonry gateposts and buttresses, which were constructed in times past, are features of South Hams scenery and you will pass many from here on. There are several near Warren Cottage. This is also a good stretch for butterflies.

After Stoke Point the drive is overgrown for a short distance but still passable and just after this a tarmac road is reached. This leads down to a caravan site (refreshments at top of hill) and the ruined but partly-restored church of St Peter the Poor Fisherman or Revelstoke church. In the 1860s the roof fell in, and for years it mouldered away, but it has now been partly re-roofed and made tidy. The church is well worth a visit, but it means a steep climb back up again. After a kilometre the drive turns inland, at Beacon Hill. The prominent ruin here is shown on Donn's map of 1765 as Membland Pleasure House. Here, after clearing a stile, the path drops steeply. Stiles and signs mark the path well to St Anchorite's Rock, a massive outcrop with an easily attained summit. Kestrels and buzzards can be seen near here.

From here on the signs are not so frequent, so make first of all for a stile at the far end of the rough pasture field, then follow the fence and cliff edge. Climb the wall and keep to the edge of cultivation. Cross the barbed wire fence near the cliff and a steep drop lands you by the Battisborough stream. Cross the stream and an equally steep climb the other side brings you to a gate. At time of writing it is necessary to turn away from the coast as no public right of way has been established along the cliffs between here and Mothecombe slipway, although it is hoped to achieve one shortly. In the meantime turn left, and follow the fence, then turn left again into a field, keeping the hedge on your right for three fields. Carry straight on at the road, and turn right at the T-junction.

(The wide bridge over the road, almost a tunnel, simply carries a private drive from one side of the estate to the other.) Near the end of the road refreshments are served at the Old School, and a private beach there is open to the public on Saturdays, Sundays and Wednesdays. Mothecombe is now just ahead.

Mothecombe belongs to the Flete estate, and because of this the Erme estuary has been preserved from every sort of proposed modern development. There cannot be a more tranquil river estuary on the whole of the south coast of England. But it isn't easy to cross to the Wonwell side (pronounced Wonnel). There is no ferry so the river has to be waded from the end of the county road across to Wonwell beach, and this can only be done with safety one hour either side of low water, and even then high winds and floodwater can make it impassable. (See Ferries and river crossings for details.) A diversion inland involves about 13 or 14 kilometres of road walking to cross the river by Sequers Bridge on the A379, so it is essential to plan your arrival at the right state of the tide. Once across the estuary, the official path is rejoined at Wonwell beach, 400 metres or so on the sea side of Wonwell slip, but it can be reached from the slipway by getting up into the woods 20 metres back from the slip and following the very obvious path south. On the right is a limekiln. It is

Butterflies:
1 Adonis Blue   4 Comma
2 High Brown Fritillary   5 Grayling
3 The Wall   6 The Brimstone

also possible to follow the beach round. Walk across the top of Wonwell beach and in front of the ruined cottages, then through a field of rough pasture to a stile. Just beyond, at Muxham Point (not marked by name on the 1:50,000 map), there is a rocky point which gives a fine view. From here to Challaborough the path is clear but strenuous, with many ups and downs. In places you are very near the cliff edge, and very much aware that protection from eternity is only an insubstantial thicket of brambles and thistles! Just west of Hoist Point, at Freshwater Bay, a small waterfall splashes to the beach from a cliff-side spring. The field above shows no evidence of stream or bog. Here, sailing craft would take on water, rather than sail for miles up an estuary.

As you near Challaborough you pass two quiet coves, Westcombe Beach and Ayrmer Cove, the latter easily reached by footpath from the beautiful village of Ringmore, 1 kilometre from the coast. Ayrmer Cove is notable for the near vertical faces of grey Dartmouth slate that

flank the strand. So glossy are these surfaces that if the sun is angled right they serve to beam their presence 6 kilometres across Bigbury Bay to Bolt Tail. Between Ayrmer Cove and Challaborough a ruined huer's hut is passed on the cliff. It was here that a watch was kept for shoals of pilchards, and when sighted a hue and cry (from the French *huer* to shout) would be made to alert the fishermen.

At the self-catering resort of Challaborough you come to the beginning of a 5-kilometre stretch of coastline from which the trappings of tourism are never far away. The impact is initially startling: fish and chips, tea bars, a multi-coloured leisure park, transistors, all jar on the soul, conditioned as it has been to peace and natural beauty for many miles.

The path now passes behind the beach, to the rear of the villas on the east side of the bay, and so on to Bigbury-on-Sea. (Youth hostel and other accommodation, and seasonal buses to Plymouth – service 99, and to Modbury – private bus service 610.) Here, the interest lies in Burgh Island, which can be reached at low tide by walking across the sands, and at high tide by using the specially-designed sea tractor. This long-legged vehicle will travel through 3 metres of water, and can cope with seas up to force 9 gale. A large hotel, now holiday flats, somewhat mars the look of Burgh Island. Nevertheless a visit is worthwhile.

The Pilchard Inn there provides refreshment, and the view from the ruined huer's hut on the summit is very rewarding. Move on a few metres from the hut and look down the sheer cliff beyond. This is one of the best places on the south coast for watching sea birds.

Back at Bigbury-on-Sea (the village of Bigbury is 3 kilometres inland) the road out is followed for 1 kilometre. At the end of the built-up area a path on the right leads down to Cockleridge and the ferry, which crosses the Avon estuary to Bantham. (At low tide it is possible to walk along the beach from the sand causeway to the ferry point and save an unpleasant section of busy road.) The ferry runs only in the season, for one hour in the morning and one hour in the afternoon, but it is possible, with great care, to wade the river at low tide. (See Ferries and river crossings, p. 106, for details). Bantham is small but it has two pubs. Like practically all the other older South Devon settlements bordering the sea it once had regular visits from sailing coasters, and the older houses and limekilns are links with these traders. Large numbers of day visitors come here and park on the Ham, the area of duneland behind the beach. (There are two buses on Wednesdays between here and Kingsbridge.)

The path now passes round the Ham on the river and sea side, but there is no reason why a short cut across the Ham shouldn't be taken to meet up with the official path by the lifeguard station at the south end of the beach.

From here the path stays between the golf course and the cliff edge until it reaches the beach by the club house. The wreck to be seen offshore at low tide is that of the Belgian ship, *Louis Sheid*, which came ashore in December 1939. This section, although tame and well-used compared with some stretches of the path, has a wide variety of plants and insects. Large areas of wild white clover, extensive patches of sea thrift, marguerite daisies and many other species are to be seen, and attract a profusion of butterflies.

From the club house the attractive village of Thurlestone, which takes its name from the pierced or 'thirled' stone in the bay, is 1 kilometre inland. Accommodation and refreshments can be found here, and there is a private bus link with Kingsbridge.

Thatched cottages in Thurlestone village

Thurlestone to Slapton Sands

(37 kilometres)

From the club house of Thurlestone golf course the path runs behind the beach, then dodges briefly inland to avoid a cliff fall. This diversion is well signposted. It rejoins the coast by the South Milton sands car park, crosses the dunes and then a long footbridge to where South Milton Ley drains into the sea. The small reed-grown valley is a nature reserve belonging to the Devon Bird Watching and Preservation Society, and with binoculars the usual freshwater habitat birds can be spotted from the bridge: reed and sedge warblers, moorhens, and herons standing motionless in the shallows.

Following the path another car park is crossed and then on to pass behind some cliff top houses, coming out on the cliffs with the coupled villages of Outer and Inner Hope ahead. From the highest point of these cliffs it is said that the Spanish Armada was first sighted in Devon, and the chain of warning beacons was begun here. Outer Hope is reached first, its fishing antecedents submerged by tourism. Then a short path going over the hill brings you to Inner Hope. Here, a diversion of 300 metres or so up the valley to the square past the coastguard cottages brings you to a charming corner of old Devon. The cluster of cottages here have changed little over the past hundred years.

Back by the beach, climb the steps by the old lifeboat station and walk out to Bolt Tail. Looking back at Inner Hope you can see how effectively the cliffs shield it from southerly gales. There is no other safe anchorage for small boats between here and the Yealm, to the west, and Salcombe, to the east. Approaching the tip of the headland you cross the fallen stone ramparts of an Iron Age promontory fort (see The imprint of man on the coast chapter).

At Bolt Tail the marks of shags and cormorants are much in evidence on the rocks below. On this headland the sea thrift, when in bloom, makes a vivid splash of Soar Mill Cove colour, and wild thyme is everywhere underfoot. You now have before you a fine stretch of cliff-top walking all the way to Salcombe, on land owned by the National Trust. So highly regarded is this section that it has been defined as heritage coast all the way to Start Point.

This coast had a deadly reputation in the pre-radar days of sail. Just east of Bolt Tail the 90-gun ship, HMS *Ramillies*, was wrecked with the loss of over 700 men. The most famous wreck in these parts was that of the four-masted Finnish barque, *Herzogin Cecilie*, which struck the Ham Stone and grounded near Soar Mill Cove in April 1936. The crew were taken off, and seven weeks later the ship was towed into Starehole Bay, near Salcombe. Here she was beached, but a sudden gale broke her back, so that she became a total loss. These are just two of many such wrecks. Between 1700 and 1972 it is known that 40 vessels were wrecked on the 7 kilometres of coast between Bolt Tail and Bolt Head.

Beyond Bolberry Down (refreshments) the path follows the crest of a rocky ridge with the cliffs on one side and a small valley running parallel on the other. Across the valley is Hazel Tor, and past Soar Mill Cove are further craggy outcrops. The rock here is mica schist, a metamorphic rock, and you will have it for company all the way to Start Point. Notice how slabs of it have been raised on edge and used as walling. Once past Soar Mill Cove the path climbs steeply, and presently a tower is seen to the left. This was once a look-out for excise men.

Bolt Head is now reached. And here you are likely to see domestic goats grazing among the outcrops. At this point the direction of travel changes suddenly. The path turns north, rounds the back of Starehole Bay, and cuts through the aptly-named Sharp Tor by the Courtenay Walk, a path hewn in the last century by the son of an Earl of Devon, Viscount Courtenay, to give access to Bolt Head. From here the view is impressive. The official path stops abreast of Sharpitor, a National Trust house, garden and museum, with youth hostel attached, but the route into Salcombe is easily traced past South and North Sands beaches. Frequent buses run between here and Kingsbridge, and there is a daily ferry service throughout the year to East Portlemouth. (See Ferries and river crossings, p. 106, for details.) (For Salcombe, see Gazetteer chapter.)

Having made the ferry crossing, turn right from the ferry steps and follow the road to Mill Bay. Take the path nearest the estuary and once again you are on National Trust land. Notice that curious parasitic plant, the dodder, growing on the gorse beside the path, its thin, red, multitudinous tendrils living off their host.

The coas
bet
Hope Cove
Thurles

Gammon Head

Looking across the estuary to a point abreast of Sharp Tor, there is a sand spit. It is marked on the map as 'The Bar'. This sand spit, at the mouth of Salcombe harbour, was a hazard to shipping, particularly at night when the tide was low, and is thought to have been the inspiration behind Tennyson's famous poem, *Crossing the Bar*.

In a short while Gara Rock Hotel (converted coastguard cottages) and its curious thatched look-out is reached, and then the path carries on to Gammon Head – probably the most photogenic of all the headlands on the South Devon coast. A crinkle-crested, thrusting spur showing as much grey rock as green grass. Tucked under its eastern flank are two beautiful sandy bays, Maceley Cove and Elender Cove, the former, particularly, being some distance from the nearest car park, is less crowded than most beaches in the peak season.

From here, Prawle Point, the southernmost tip of Devon, is reached. Prawle means 'look-out hill', and it must have been a vantage point for possible invaders or ships returning after long voyages from early times. (An occasional private bus serves East Prawle, $1\frac{1}{2}$ kilometres inland.) The path passes near the coastguard hut, then heads back towards the line of coastguard cottages. It follows the sea side of the hedge in front of the cottages, then makes off along the low cliffs, following the edge of cultivation.

Corm

Gannet with y

VANA

47

Turnstones

At Prawle Point the scenery has changed dramatically. East of Prawle is another section of raised beach such as was seen near Wembury. The original cliffs are the width of one field back from the edge of the sea, and display an interesting array of sculptured shapes as you move along. Here, too, you see more stone slabs on edge forming field boundaries, and slab stiles worn smooth with use are another feature of this stretch.

From now on the path is straightforward, and remote from contact with cars until Lannacombe Beach is reached.

The next bay is Great Mattiscombe Sand (pronounced Matchcombe), and the landmarks here are the Pinnacles: isolated rock stacks on the shore formed of deposits of glacial head on schist bases. The beach here is popular with holidaymakers as cars can be driven quite close, but swimmers should not venture far out as a treacherous tidal race formed by the innocuously named Peartree Point is only just off the headland. The path goes right round the Point, bringing you very close to the elemental force of the sea. Unless it happens to be low tide a line of very disturbed water can be seen. The shattered nature of the frost-split cliff reflects the wildness of the scene, and as you round the corner Start Point lighthouse comes into view, a reminder of the hazards of this part of the coast.

The path follows the clifftop to Start Point doubling back to descend to the Trinity House road which leads to the lighthouse. If time allows and the lighthouse is open, a visit is well worthwhile. It was built in 1836, and the light has a range of 20·8 miles. As you would expect, this is a good place to watch birds. The word Start is derived from the Anglo-Saxon 'Steort' meaning a tail, an element also found in the name of the bird, the redstart.

Beyond Start Point the path leads to the road away from the lighthouse. Abreast of the car park it crosses a slab stile, and then gently descends a bracken-covered slope towards Hallsands. This is a good place to take in the landscape change which has occurred since Start Point was rounded. The prickly rock exposures of mica schist rock are left behind as you enter the belt of Meadfoot beds, a mainly slate type of rock, and much more susceptible to erosion. The view onwards gives the impression of a very regular simple coastline, but this has not always been the case. In Ice Age times when the sea level was higher, the English Channel penetrated the several shallow valleys which are now blocked off by shingle barriers. The headlands, too, projected further. A complicated interaction of climatic changes, waves and deposition has brought about the present coastline and, aided by man's intervention, the process of change continues to the present day.

Meddling with the natural order of things caused the death of Hallsands, the first small settlement you reach going north from Start Point. Until the early years of this century its thirty-seven houses stood in a row above the beach, secure on their rocky ledge, protected by a shingle foreshore. In 1897 a contractor engaged in construction work at Devonport Dockyard was given permission to dredge shingle offshore at Hallsands. In a very short time nearly 500,000 tons was taken, and the beach level dropped 4 metres before dredging stopped in 1902. Its natural defences dissipated, the village was exposed to the sea, and in a succession of storms all the houses were demolished, save one. The last, and most destructive, was in January 1917 when twenty-four houses were wrecked. A few houses were built at Greenstraight for the displaced inhabitants of Hallsands, mostly from money donated to a public appeal, but the whole affair, from the granting of the dredging licence to the failure to provide compensation, is an appalling example of official ineptitude. You can divert slightly from the path to see the ruins of Hallsands, and then pass on to Greenstraight (refreshments). It was from the withy beds behind the beach that the Hallsands fishermen got their willow rods to make lobster and crab pots.

The path now passes over Tinsey Head and down to Beesands. It too has had its share of tragedy, as it was hit by German hit-and-run aircraft during the last war. At the southern end of the settlement there are some old cottages and a pub, but the northern end of Beesands is a sprawl of caravans. Through these you have to walk making your way past another withy bed; its name, Widdicombe Ley, defining its use since Domesday.

Start Point

From Beesands Cellars, an indication of fish curing in a place-name, the path winds up a wooded lane to make a detour round a deep quarry, then drops steeply down to Torcross. (If walking in the other direction, take the signposted path from the public lavatories behind the Torcross Hotel.) Torcross is a pleasant village, with shops, accommodation and a regular bus service to Dartmouth and Kingsbridge. Indeed, unless you are keen to stride along beside the A379 for 3½ kilometres to Strete Gate at the north end of Slapton Sands, a bus ride will get you from one end to the other in about 12 minutes, calling at Slapton village on the way. The A379 dates only from 1864, when a turnpike road was built along 'The Line', as Slapton Sands is known locally. Formerly it was rough grazing for cattle, with a fence and a gate at the northern end to prevent straying – hence Strete Gate.

The official path takes you to the verge between the road and Slapton Ley, the most extensive natural freshwater lake in Devon. The Ley is a privately-owned nature reserve, leased to the Field Studies Council. A Field Centre for research and education is sited between the Reserve and the village, and 2,000 students a year pass through its doors. The Field Centre produces leaflets about the natural history of the South Hams, and a programme of guided walks is undertaken from June to September. The visitor who prefers to learn things for himself will find the two nature trail booklets useful. The shingle and pebble banks of Chesil Beach in Dorset and of Slapton, Greenstraight and Beesands have their

50

origin in the period just after the last Ice Age when the glaciers melted, the sea rose and swept all before it to form the beaches and barriers of the present coast. Hitherto the rising land behind Slapton Ley was the coastline. The freshwater of the Ley now provides a valuable educational resource through its aquatic life and marginal plants. And just across the road is the beach and the sea with opportunities for studying the progression from constant sea-water immersion to occasional spray contact. The area is also noted for a contribution it made to the Allied effort in the last war.

In 1943 Slapton Sands was chosen by the Americans for beach landing practice, in readiness for the Normandy invasion. Because live ammunition was being used, it meant that a large part of the hinterland had to be evacuated for the safety of the inhabitants. In six weeks 3,000 people, their animals and belongings were moved from 30,000 acres in seven parishes. This was at a time when transport and petrol were hard to come by, when most of the able-bodied men were in the Services and when the days were short and the weather bad.

Inevitably when the firing started there was damage, but remarkably little. Visiting the delightful village of Slapton today it is impossible to imagine a time when its houses were deserted, when rats scuttled untroubled round the streets and gnawed the putty in the window frames, and when no birds sang.

A reminder of this period is a stone memorial obelisk standing beside the coast path near the turning to Slapton. It was erected by the Americans and unveiled by General Grunther in 1954.

There are other reminders. A hole was blown in the wall of the Church House Inn at Stokenham and is still a talking point among customers. Many trees in the impact area are too full of shrapnel to be any use as timber. And on the landward side of Slapton Sands a system of trenches can still be followed.

Slapton Sands to Starcross

(63 kilometres)

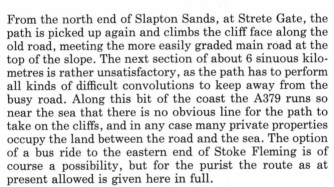

From the north end of Slapton Sands, at Strete Gate, the path is picked up again and climbs the cliff face along the old road, meeting the more easily graded main road at the top of the slope. The next section of about 6 sinuous kilometres is rather unsatisfactory, as the path has to perform all kinds of difficult convolutions to keep away from the busy road. Along this bit of the coast the A379 runs so near the sea that there is no obvious line for the path to take on the cliffs, and in any case many private properties occupy the land between the road and the sea. The option of a bus ride to the eastern end of Stoke Fleming is of course a possibility, but for the purist the route as at present allowed is given here in full.

Just over 100 metres east of the top of the old road, on the opposite side, a gate is entered. Follow up the hedge and turn right through another gate and along a track which comes out on a wide side road to a T-junction near Strete church where there is a youth hostel. Turn right here, and then left, down a lane, passing the Tallis Rock Hotel, coming out on the main road at the east end of Strete. This busy traffic route must now be followed for about 500 metres. Turn left at the lane signed 'Southwood', right at the fork, and right at the next junction. This brings you onto the main road at Blackpool Sands, an attractive cove bearing no resemblance to its north-country namesake. Here, the local people repulsed a Breton invasion force in 1404.

Turn away from the coast and the main road just east of the bridge over the stream, and follow the by-road for half a kilometre, then turn right up a steep and rocky track signposted 'Public Bridleway'. This leads directly to Stoke Fleming church, which is well worth visiting for a look at its splendid brass of John Corp (1361), the oldest dated brass in the west, and that of his grand-daughter, Elyenore (1391). In the churchyard is the grave of George Parker Bidder (1806–78), who was born in Moreton-hampstead and became famous as 'The Calculating Boy'.

Slapton Ley and the beach beyond

From an early age he could perform complicated mathematical computations in his head. Cecil Torr in his *Small Talk at Wreyland*, First Series, 1918, recorded how Bidder could find the cube root of 304, 821, 217 instantaneously, the cube root of 67, 667, 921, 875 in $\frac{1}{4}$ minute, and that of 897, 339, 273, 974, 902, 153 in $2\frac{1}{2}$ minutes. In due course he became a nationally-known civil engineer, and was associated with Robert Stephenson in the London to Birmingham railway, and responsible for the construction of the Victoria Docks in London.

Opposite the churchyard gate take the road heading north. At the end of the road you will find a gate marked, 'Footpath. Pedestrians Only', which passes between the enclosures of a privately-owned exotic bird sanctuary. Turn right here, then immediately left. This brings you to the main road again, but you simply cross it and enter a lane at Windward Cottage, which you follow for just over a kilometre until you reach the National Trust car park at Little Dartmouth. Climb the stile here and follow the signposted path towards the coast, observing the amusingly ambiguous notice which warns 'Sheep! Please keep dogs under control'. Thanks are due to the Devon Women's Institutes for this stretch of the path being open, for it was they who raised the money for its purchase. The path for the next 2 kilometres is truly delightful. Glorious views open up ahead of the still-forbidden Scabbacombe coast topped by the prominent Day Mark, a hollow limestone tower about 25 metres high erected by Dartmouth Harbour Commissioners in 1864. This is a rewarding section of the path to observe birds, as the route switchbacks down to Compass Cove and crosses a sea gulley by a footbridge before climbing round Blackstone Point and running into Dartmouth through pleasant shaded woodland above the castle. (For Dartmouth, see Gazetteer chapter.)

After arriving at Kingswear from Dartmouth by the lower ferry it is worth walking a little way up the road approach to see the Kingswear terminus of the Torbay Steam Railway. This privately-run system is operated on authentic Great Western Railway lines between here and Paignton during the season.

Back at the ferry slip the route of the coast path is under the nearby arch, up Alma Steps and then turning right to go along Beacon Road. The road becomes a footpath, then a private road and turns inland. As already hinted, this section of coast, some 8 kilometres as the would-be path runs, is not yet a right of way. The lack of access to this stretch is particularly unfortunate as it is rated highly in landscape terms. About 7 kilometres hereabouts are defined as heritage coast.

Where a fork appears ahead, bear right slightly downhill and turn right over a footbridge just before a white cottage

Blackpool Sands, near Dartmouth

is reached. The way is now up a rocky path and straight on through Brownstone farmyard along a tarmac road. Eventually a T-junction is reached by a small copse. Turn right here and follow Scabbacombe Lane until it becomes a stony track and ends at Man Sands. A limekiln here is a reminder of the time when coasting vessels put in at Man Sands to unload Berry Head limestone, and a line of converted coastguard cottages overlooking the beach is yet another reminder of the trade in duty evasion in the eighteenth and nineteenth centuries which led to the formation of the Coastguard Service.

The coast path now hugs the sea to Berry Head $3\frac{1}{2}$ kilometres ahead, and first climbs the steep and lofty Southdown Cliff before contouring round to Sharkham Point. From here the sudden transition to limestone at Durl Head is very noticeable, as are the numerous chalet villages on the cliff tops, telling you that you are now approaching the Torbay holiday area. The coast path here is much used by holiday-makers, and it is good to see people walking between the beach pleasures of St. Mary's Bay and the assertive foreland of Berry Head.

The limestone belt is entered at Durl Head, a feature seen from across the bay, and if you have a head for heights it is worth going out on a rocky ridge here to see the cliffs fall away on either side.

Dartmouth Upper Ferry crossing the River Dart

The River Dart and part of Dartmouth Castle

Soon the wall surrounding one of Berry Head's forts is reached, and then on into Berry Head Country Park, which is administered by Torbay Borough Council. The excellent 30-page official guide to Berry Head can be bought from the car park kiosk and is recommended. It contains many detailed maps and illustrations. Also worth getting is a nature trail leaflet with identification sketches of some of the limestone-tolerant plants found in the area. There is so much to see here that you would do well to allow a couple of hours for exploration. There are the plants; so different to those seen previously on the path, because of the limestone sub-strata. And there is an unrestricted view of the sea birds from the cliff top, since the edges fall away so steeply to the sea. Berry Head thrusts out so far into the sea that gannets can sometimes be seen diving for fish. The fulmar too, with its graceful, soaring, stiff-winged flight is often observed. For hundreds of years the limestone was quarried on the north side of the promontory, but work ceased in 1969. The scope of the operation can be judged by looking over the wall at the enormous bite taken out of the Head.

Limestone, of course, means caves, and the Ash Hole Cavern (not open to the public) on the approaches to Berry Head from Brixham revealed bones of reindeer and oxon overlain by remains of a Roman era. Near where cars are now parked were found flint arrowheads and scrapers. In Iron Age times the local tribe built a defensive earthwork across the neck of the headland, and as recently as 1800 this was 6 metres high. It was this feature which gave the Head its name. Berry is a corruption of Byri or Byrig, the Saxon word for castle or fortification. This place-name element has suffered another mutation to be found in the name Brixham.

The present fortifications, capable of accommodating 40 guns, were built in 1803, during the Napoleonic Wars, but they were not needed. However, Bonaparte did put into Torbay – as a prisoner on board HMS *Bellerophon* – en route to St. Helena!

Apart from being interested in the early nineteenth century forts, visitors to Berry Head are also interested in the coastguard station, which is manned all day and every day, and the curiously squat lighthouse nearby. Standing, as this lighthouse does, high on the cliff top any additional height is unnecessary. The revolving lantern is controlled by a weight hung in a shaft 50 metres deep beneath the lighthouse.

A little further inland is a science fiction type structure which is an aircraft navigational beacon, and beside the gate near the café is a cloud-level determining device. The Royal Observer Corps also has a presence on this headland. But it is because of its quality as a view point that so many people visit Berry Head. On a very clear day Portland Bill, in Dorset, is just visible 56 kilometres to the east, and much of South Devon can be seen curving around Lyme Bay. Frequently one can see super-tankers lying several miles out waiting to be lightened by smaller tankers or awaiting orders to proceed, depending on

Fishing boats in Brixham harbour

market prices. A coin-operated telescope is provided for anyone without binoculars. The café here serves light meals.

The way down into Brixham from Berry Head is sign-posted and the road is reached near the Berry Head House Hotel where an enormous, roofless, wartime fuel-storage tank serves as a car park. What is now the hotel was the hospital for the garrison up on Berry Head, and was later lived in by the Rev. H F Lyte of 'Abide with me' fame.

From here the road into Brixham is clear and direct. (For Brixham, see Gazetteer chapter.) From the western side of Brixham harbour you make your way through Freshwater quarry car- and dinghy-park. On reaching the end you round the point and come into Fishcombe Cove, a pleasant inlet. Take the steps to the beach (refreshments), go up the wooded lane at the head of the beach and then turn right where a sign reads, 'Broadsands – 1 hour'. Your way now passes between two holiday camps and down to another small beach, Churston Cove. Cross the top of the strand and climb the path which ascends the ridge between the cove and the sea. This brings you to a long, straight stretch which is something like a green corridor. Behind the fence on one side can be heard the reactions of golfers to hooks and slices, while on the other side, is the almost continuous whine of outboard motors, as this corner of Torbay is set aside for water-skiers. But there isn't much to see.

Eventually the path zig-zags down to Elbury (Elberry) Cove. At the south end of the beach is the ruined private bathing station of the Bullers of Lupton House, a prominent Devon family, 2 kilometres inland. A freshwater spring bubbles up into the sea offshore, but can only be seen on very calm days. Carry on along the top of the beach, round the grassy headland and down to reach Broadsands (refreshments). The sea wall should now be followed to a point just beyond halfway round the beach where a path should be taken leading under the railway viaduct. Having passed under the viaduct, turn right and follow what is a clear and manicured path all the way to Goodrington.

The official coast path ends here, not to begin again until Hope's Nose, east of Torquay. Buses to Torquay are frequent and can be taken if desired, but if you prefer to stay on foot there is a route near the sea most of the way.

From Goodrington this route takes you first along the sea front, then onto a zig-zag path up to Roundham Gardens, and along a tarmac path around the Head to join Cliff Road which leads to Paignton harbour. (For Paignton, see Gazetteer chapter.) Leaving Paignton esplanade, and where the road turns left, the rising path to Hollicombe Head is direct and quiet. Soon, however, there is no alternative but to meet the main Paignton to Torquay road which has to be your route for the 2½ kilometres to Torquay harbour. (For Torquay, see Gazetteer chapter.) The best way out of Torquay is to walk along Victoria Parade from the Strand where the road climbs past the Imperial Hotel, and to turn in just after the hotel. This leads to Rock End from which there is a fine panorama around Torbay to Berry Head. The way continues, turning left to ascend a flight of steps and then onto a path that winds up and down through the Rock End estate, past a profusion of flowering shrubs, which grant a real Mediterranean touch to the scene. Seats are conveniently placed at intervals along the way. Eventually the path comes out on the airy open space of Daddyhole Plain. (Daddyhole takes its name from a cave in the cliff; the home of a 'Daddy' or demon.)

The route descends to Meadfoot sea road through a wooded grove, and the sea wall can now be followed to the far end. When first reaching the wall look out for a piped spring trickling through the limestone cliff on the opposite side of the road. People come here from miles around to collect drinking water believing it to have qualities beneficial to health. At the far end of Meadfoot sea road a path cuts through a corner of the car park here and climbs to Ilsham Marine Drive. Hereabouts, the evergreen holm oak and dominating Kilmorie flats are significant features of the landscape.

Opposite Thatcher Rock the official path is regained, and

loops briefly seawards and back again on to Ilsham Marine Drive further on. Although only a short section it should on no account be omitted, as you get quite near to Thatcher Rock, and there is a wonderful feeling of being close to the elements. A plaque near where the path leaves Ilsham Marine Drive notes that this 7½ acres of open land – Hillway Close – was given anonymously in 1968 for public enjoyment.

Back on Marine Drive the road must be followed briefly – by taking a turning on the right a diversion can be made to Hope's Nose, a favourite spot for fishing off the rocks. The coast path now runs parallel with the road on the higher side for several hundred metres. Where it meets up with the road again, cross it and follow the Bishop's Walk round Black Head. Bishop's Walk is so-called because a nineteenth century Bishop of Exeter, Henry Phillpotts, who lived nearby for many years at Bishopstowe, now the Palace Hotel, made this walk his own. In places it has been blasted out of the dolerite and seats have now been discreetly placed to make the most of the views. After rounding Black Head a change in geology becomes visible ahead. There is the limestone promontory of Long Quarry Point, denuded by years of quarrying, with the red sandstone cliffs beyond. At the

Paignton harbour

View from a spot near Petit Tor Point, looking towards Babbacombe

end of the Bishop's Walk the road is reached by way of Anstey's Cove car park, and has to be followed for 150 metres before steps take you up and onto the path leading to Babbacombe Downs and Walls Hill. Make for the northern corner of this pleasant open space, when the way down to Babbacombe Beach becomes obvious. There is a small quay here, refreshments and a few houses at sea level. The area has given its name to a man convicted of a local murder in 1884, who subsequently became known as, 'The man they couldn't hang'. John 'Babbacombe' Lee, the footman of a Miss Keyse, an elderly lady found with her throat cut and skull fractured after a fire, was sentenced to death by hanging in Exeter. However, on three occasions the gallows failed to work when the lever was operated, and the Home Secretary commuted the sentence to 'life'. He was eventually released in 1907, married, and is thought to have died in the USA in 1933.

The next bit of path to Oddicombe Beach is at sea level, and if an easterly wind is blowing and the tide is high you are likely to get showered with spray. Oddicombe Beach (refreshments) has a cliff railway dating from 1926, and it is most interesting to watch it in operation. The coast path underpasses the railway halfway up and climbs steeply to Petit Tor before contouring some wooded slopes and crossing the road leading down to Watcombe Beach. It carries on up the other side of the valley and presently enters the Valley of Rocks, a strange green bowl which could be a pantomime stage set or a backdrop for *A Midsummer Night's Dream*. One expects to see pixies sitting on the ivy-covered boulders.

The path takes you out of this enchanting fairy dell onto a ledge hacked out of a cliff, but a handrail gives security. Soon Rockhouse Lane is reached, and the attractive village of Maidencombe (refreshments). In the front garden of one of the thatched houses is a Judas tree (*Cercis Siliquastrum*) which is preserved as of special botanical interest, and is supported by a wooden prop.

The next 2½ kilometres to Labrador Bay are tough walking. Up and down most of the way, as the path climbs and descends the sides of a series of hanging valleys between field fences and the cliff edge. Not only is it a switchback path, but also a bramble-snatching path, and shorts are simply not suitable here. Because of the plant growth this is a rewarding stretch for naturalists. Butterflies, in particular, are abundant.

Eventually you reach Labrador Bay, named after a house built here by a Captain Trapp, an eighteenth century North American trader. The house has long-since gone.

Part of the beach at Teignmouth

Teignmouth: looking across The Salty to the docks beyond

The busy A379 runs close to the coast here and, to avoid clifftop development, it is necessary to turn inland, following the path along the main road and then behind the roadside hedge bank to a stile. From here the path follows the hedge on the right down past a pitch-and-putt course and up on to the Ness: Teignmouth, the coast eastwards, and the Teign estuary are laid out before you during the descent. At the top of the Ness, turn left and the way is clear down to Shaldon (refreshments, and frequent buses at the south end of Shaldon Bridge). (If walking the path in the other direction, climb the Ness leaving all buildings to your right.) The ferry to Teignmouth leaves from the beach. Be careful to join the ferry and not a boat going out to sea for two hours fishing as a Dutch tourist did recently! (For Teignmouth, see Gazetteer chapter.)

From the beach on the Teignmouth side of the estuary there is no official coast path for the next 6 kilometres. You can catch a 186/187 bus from Teignmouth to Dawlish if you wish, but there is a good walking route for much of the way, which is now given.

Only if the tide is low can the promenade be followed, northwards. This then becomes a sea wall, with the beach to the right, the main Paddington to Penzance railway line to the left, and the cliffs above. Where the wall ends near the first of a series of tunnels between here and Dawlish it becomes an underpass beneath the railway below high tide level, hence the warning at the beginning of this paragraph to be aware of the tide before setting out on this stretch. If, when you get to the far end, you find the path under water, the only thing to do, unless the tide is ebbing, is to return and take the road, or at least the path between the road and the cliff, which means a considerable climb and detour.

Assuming the tide is low, you will now climb Smugglers' Lane to Holcombe where the main road is reached. Turn right, and follow it for just over 1 kilometre. At the top of the hill above Dawlish, opposite Coronation Avenue, you can turn in to a small cliff-top park which leads to a zig-zag path heading down to the mouth of the most northerly of several railway tunnels. This sea wall railway, one of the most interesting lengths of line to travel on in Great Britain, was engineered by Isambard Kingdom Brunel, and reached Teignmouth in 1846. The names of the tunnels along it from south to north are: Parson tunnel, Clerk tunnel, Phillott tunnel, Coryton tunnel and Kennaway tunnel. The first two names are taken from the sandstone sea stacks off Holcombe, and the other three are named after the landowners through whose estates the tunnels were driven. (For Dawlish, see Gazetteer chapter.)

Once at the sea wall at Dawlish it is possible to follow it all the way to Dawlish Warren, some 3 kilometres, but again this can only be done if the tide is low and the sea calm. This time the constraint is just beyond Dawlish station where a low-level length of path forces you to take another route if the conditions are wrong.

If you can't follow the sea wall you should go up the A379 out of Dawlish onto the Exeter road, and at the point where the road bears away inland about 1 kilometre from Dawlish a footpath sign near the Rockstone Hotel indicates the way to go. This is the official path.

Dawlish Warren (refreshments) is a popular, self-catering family holiday resort to which many people from Exeter come on day trips, and it is here that the official path once again comes to an end. There is no way across to Exmouth from here, and it is necessary to walk 3 kilometres to Starcross to catch the seasonal ferry. The alternative is to get a train or bus to Exeter and come down to Exmouth the same way, but the method of crossing must depend on your inclination and the time available.

The walk to Starcross is unpleasant, although Cockwood, an old-world backwater is interesting. Still standing at Starcross, is the Italianate sandstone tower which housed one of the stationary engines built by Brunel to power his railway, a system that ran on 'atmospheric' principles.

A continuous pipe with a longitudinal slot on top was laid between the rails in which ran a piston fitted to the leading vehicle of a train. The stationary engines pumped out air from the pipe in front of the piston forming a

The sea wall on the way to Dawlish Warren

vacuum while air coming in behind the piston pushed the train along.

The system was not successful, and after spending £426,368 installing what became known as the 'atmospheric caper' Brunel cut his losses and began running conventional locomotives. The idea is perpetuated in the name of an inn at Starcross – the 'Atmospheric Railway'.

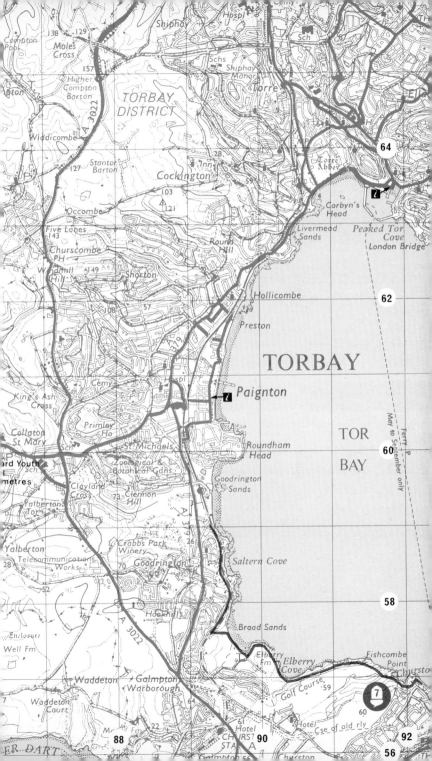

Steps Bridge Youth Hostel
20 kilometres

B 3381
Easter Hill 56
Southbrook
Cofford R
Fm
Nesswood
Cockwood
Cofton
Edstdon
Eastdon Ho
Shutterton
Shutterton Br
Hospl
Langdon Ho
Gatehouse
DAWLISH EAST
Sch
DAWLISH WEST
Lussombe Castle
Allen Fm
Cemy
Southwood Fm
Oaklands Park
Westbrook Fm
PH
Holcombe Down
Holcombe
The Parson and Clerk
Sprey Point
TEIGNMOUTH
Pier
The Salty
Shaldon
The Ness Ho
Hotel

Sturcross
Ferry
Great Bull Hill
Golf Links
Dawlish Warren
CH
Dawlish Warren
Hotel
Langstone Rock
Breakwater
CG Lookout
DAWLISH
Breakwater
Coryton's Cove
Horse Cove

New House Fm
Gulliford
Pitt Fm
Hensford
Langdon Barton
Millcroft Fm
Langdon Ho
Lower Rixdale Fm

80

78

76

74

72

94   9   96   98

The front at Dawlish

The pier at Starcro

Starcross to
Lyme Regis

(42 kilometres)

No other section of the South Devon Coast Path is so self-contained as the East Devon stretch from Exmouth to the Dorset border near Lyme Regis.

The Exe estuary is a bold barrier and truly separates East Devon from the rest of the county. The rocks on either side of the Exe are the same – the rich, rosy red of the new red sandstone – but they are not powerful enough to unify the scene. It is on this section of the path that your way is straightforward and free of ferry crossings. This stretch is very much a unity.

If you have crossed from Starcross you will land at Exmouth Dock. (For Exmouth, see Gazetteer chapter.) From here walk along the promenade for 1½ kilometres. At Foxholes café and car park walk up Foxholes Road for a short distance, then take the tarmac path which climbs gently above the eastern end of the sea front. On reaching the coastguard look-out it is worth stopping to look at the splendid view across the mouth of the estuary. Approaching the High Land of Orcombe (National Trust) a stone-slotted gate post is passed. This used to be a common way of securing animals in fields in upland Britain, but stone gate posts are not often met with in lowland areas. Instead of a hinged gate, slip bars were used, one for each slot. They were always used in pairs, so perhaps its twin is the one I saw lying on the ground, face down? If so, this one should have a more sophisticated type of slot to its partner; maybe an 'L'-shaped slot. This kind of gate is frequently seen on eastern Dartmoor, and there are some on the Dorset Coast Path. At this spot it is often possible to hear the bell buoy ringing out to sea; it is visible from the High Land of Orcombe, marking the entrance to Exmouth fairway.

Now the Sandy Bay caravan site comes into view (refreshments) and the Royal Marine rifle range on Straight Point. The line of the path is clear; it runs outside the range fence across the neck of the Point, and

75

Powderham Castle. near Starcross. Home of the Earls of Devon since about 1390

soon picks up the cliffs again. There follows a climb to the top of West Down (129 metres) where there is a triangulation point by the path, and a quite superb view in all directions. Here the East Devon pebble beds begin.

The path carries on downhill into Budleigh Salterton, and the sea front can be followed to the car park at the far end. (For Budleigh Salterton, see Gazetteer chapter.) On the way, stop awhile to watch the Budleigh fishermen still carrying on in the traditional way. On the top of the shingle beach are the man-powered capstans used for hauling the clinker-built boats up the steep slope, and the wooden rollers for easing their passage.

Unfortunately there is no footbridge across the mouth of the river Otter although the distance is small – just a few metres. Because of this, a 2-kilometre detour inland has to be made. On reaching the car park, head inland towards the cricket pavilion, then follow the flood bank to the first crossing point over the river, White Bridge. This walk along the bank of the river gives you an opportunity to observe the estuary birds without disturbing them, as the trees and shrubs beside the path serve to conceal your presence. So from this point of view the necessary detour into a marshy habitat is welcome, and adds variety to the walk. There haven't been many opportunities since Slapton to see wildlife and flora at close quarters. Cross White Bridge and pass down the eastern side of the estuary on the field side of the hedge. The curlew can often be heard along here.

At Otterton Point the path reaches the cliffs once more, and the next 3 kilometres to Ladram Bay are pleasant and easy. Brandy Head is a smugglers' place name: East Devon had a thriving smuggling trade in the eighteenth and nineteenth centuries.

Ladram Bay (refreshments) supports another caravan site behind its wooded valley. Those who visit the beach here are thrown together in cramped confusion, especially at high tide; the Bay is too small for the summer population it attracts. Offshore there are several impressive sandstone sea stacks, all bearing summit evidence that they have been climbed – but how?

There now follows a stern climb almost from sea level to 157 metres up to the top of Peak Hill, that is if you are prepared to thrash your way through the conifer and bramble jungle to the crowning trig point.

The coast path contours round the north side, short of the top, but several paths lead off through the plantation in the general direction of upwards, and you have only to follow one of these eventually to arrive, scratched and bleeding, at the top. It is worth bearing in mind while

Sailing on the Exe estuary near Exmouth

Hayes Barton farmhouse, East Budleigh. Birthplace of Sir Walter Raleigh

you are catching your breath that you have climbed one quarter of the height of the highest hill on Dartmoor, and that means in the whole of southern England. There are a couple of superior points beyond Sidmouth, but this is the highest cliff top so far on the South Devon Coast Path. To descend, reverse the process in the opposite direction, but not down the face of the cliff! A prehistoric hill-top or camp is now mostly gone, either over the edge, or submerged in vegetation, but a 1964 excavation showed it to have been occupied in Neolithic times, say about 3000 BC, and also during the Dark Ages, about AD 500.

From High Peak the route is clear and falls and climbs again to the seaward end of Mutter's Moor, one of the East Devon greensand plateaux. The flints underfoot are yet another geological mutation. Mutter was the name of a smuggler in the 1840s who operated out of Exmouth.

The way down is through a grove of beech trees and out on to Peak Hill Road. Some 300 metres down the hill you can ease your feet by treading a broad, grassy strip until you are nearly into Sidmouth. (If walking east to west, turn off at Peak Hill Road just after the thatched Peak Hill Cottage.) (For Sidmouth, see Gazetteer chapter.)

Sidmouth sea front, where the fishing boats run up on the pebbles and the red cliffs beyond make a pleasing still-life subject, should now be followed to the eastern end of the town. The river Sid is crossed by footbridge and then the steep climb up Salcombe Hill begins. On the way up there is a Devon Trust for Nature Conservation sign on the right. These East Devon cliffs support a rich variety of plant and bird life. Steep enough to deter human predators, but able to give root to small wind-stunted ash, blackthorn, hawthorn and holly. Bramble and ivy smother everything, making a natural bird sanctuary. Yellow-hammers, bullfinches and green woodpeckers are often seen, but the grasshopper warbler, which also inhabits the area, is more likely to be heard than seen. Its call is a single, high note, rather like the sound of an angler's reel when being wound in.

In ascending Salcombe Hill you are at first treading on a soft, chalky, red clay called marl, and here and there flints occur. These have been washed down from the flinty layer on the summit. Where the slope gets steeper the greensand is reached. This is a hard sandstone, unproductive agriculturally, and often allowed to find its own climax as a heather and gorse heath. Modern estate management now plants these areas with conifers; hence the plantation on the top of Peak Hill. From the top of Salcombe Hill, it is thought provoking to look across and see how modern Sidmouth has sprawled back 3 kilometres to Sidford. To the north-west the Sidmouth Gap provides

Sidmouth beach

Budleigh Salterton beach

Otterton village

Yellowhammer

the main access from the Exeter direction by road, and the railway (now defunct) also came through this natural break in the greensand plateau. A memorial stone is now reached which reads: 'South Combe Farm, including most of Salcombe Hill, dedicated as an open space. Vaughan Cornish, 1937'. A little further on is a large chunk of greensand called the Frog Stone. This rock was lifted from Hook Ebb to its present position by a Royal Navy Wessex helicopter in 1964 at the instigation of the Sid Vale Association to provide a signpost or reference point. The wave-erosion scallops on its surface betray its sojourn on the beach. It was near here that a particularly nasty incident occurred during a smuggling run early last century. A cargo of brandy kegs was being hauled up the cliff by smugglers, and one of a party of coastguards grabbed the end of the rope and was hauled up with the last keg. When his face appeared over the edge the smugglers cut the rope and he fell to his death down the cliff.

The path now dips steeply to Salcombe Mouth, jinks inland, and climbs again to the National Trust land of Higher Dunscombe Cliff. Soon the path veers away from the cliff edge through a tumbled landscape of flinty hummocks. These are the discarded heaps of flint left over from lime-burning operations over hundreds of years. At this point you have to descend to the pebbles at Weston Mouth to gain the other side of the valley, but the effort is well worthwhile. Cars cannot get near this lonely beach, so even in mid-summer the crowds are absent. Off season, and especially when a gale is blowing, the scene is awe-inspiring. Waves crash on the pebbles sending spray across the beach to drench the half-dozen summer chalets which cower under what are the highest cliffs on this path. Fishermen once kept boats here, and a rusty capstan can be seen almost swamped by brambles.

Their huts have now been converted into small holiday homes.

From the east side of the small stream which reaches the beach the path climbs steeply to the top of the cliff. At the National Trust sign 'Weston Cliff' the path bears half left away from the coast, and for about the next 3 kilometres you are out of sight of the sea. After diagonally crossing the first field after the National Trust sign the path keeps a line of hedges on its left until it meets a flint track going straight on. This is followed, still in the same direction, taking the left turn at the fork and becoming a stiled path through a wood. Between the trees the fine parish church of Branscombe can be seen. The path eventually comes out on the hill above Branscombe Mouth (refreshments, and number 497 bus up the valley). Away to the left stretches the straggling but attractive village of Branscombe, and below is a row of converted coastguard cottages and a public car park just behind the beach. Once on the hill and beyond Branscombe Mouth there is a choice of paths. You can climb to the top of the hill – yet another steep ascent – or pass through the cliff-side caravan site here and take the landslip path. My preference, and I have done both, is for the latter. Sated by now with cliff-top views the undercliff path offers something different. The caravan site occupies the potato patches where generations of local men raised crops within a stone's throw of the sea. Pannier baskets on donkeys' backs were used to carry the potatoes home. The path takes the higher track through the caravans, and soon becomes a narrow footpath under menacing chalk cliffs, the most westerly chalk outcrop in Britain. You are now in the Hooken landslip, which broke away from the mainland mass in 1790.

Ahead are the Pinnacles, looking like a ruined hilltop castle. The path dips and climbs and passes enormous chalk blocks which have broken away from the cliff in

Seaton beach

The harbour at Lyme Regis

times past. Looking back as the path climbs up between the cliff face and the Pinnacles there appears to be a cave opening halfway up the cliff. This is an adit in connection with the Beer stone quarry which is mostly underground and reached from opencast workings 1½ kilometres to the north. The adit followed the best of the Beer stone levels and was exposed when the cliff fell away.

Beer stone was known to the Romans, but came into its own in the Middle Ages, during the time of great church and cathedral building. It is said that when first split from bed rock it can be sawn with a carpenter's saw, but it hardens after exposure to the air. The path now climbs steeply and joins the cliff top alternative just west of Beer Head. (If you favoured the cliff top alternative from Branscombe Mouth, the path takes you up a lung blowing slope and follows the cliff edge, on the way passing the old coastguard look-out.)

From the Beer Head coastguard look-out a fresh view opens up eastwards. Beer itself is tucked in 1 kilometre ahead, and Seaton occupies the low-lying sea frontage at the mouth of the river Axe. Beyond, stretches the wooded slopes of Bindon and Dowlands landslips, with Lyme Regis and the eastern end of the South Devon Coast Path a few kilometres out of sight 'round the corner'. The cliff edge is now followed going towards Beer, and presently a large caravan site to the left comes into view. This bit of the path is much used by the large summer intake of tourists, so that it requires an effort of the imagination to see this coast as a lonely stretch of southern England. But because of this relative remoteness the smuggling fraternity of East Devon were as active as any in the South-West. One character in particular has passed

A glimpse of the beach at the fishing village of Beer

into local folklore as the 'Rob Roy of the West' – Jack Rattenbury of Beer, whose smuggling career stretched from 1794 to 1835.

The path is clear going eastwards, and after passing along Little Lane the route drops down into Beer. (If walking westwards, turn into Little Lane opposite Beer coastguard houses at the top of Common Lane.) There is a youth hostel here. (For Beer see Gazetteer chapter.)

Leave Beer by the lower path option. Looking back it is noticeable how the beach there is protected from westerly gales by Beer Head, and how rain and wind have pitted the chalk cliffs. A stroll of 1 kilometre brings you to Seaton, the last descent into the tarmac road of the town being down a flight of wooden steps. (If walking from east to west these steps are 150 metres up the hill from the lavatories at the western end of Seaton sea front.) (For Seaton, see Gazetteer chapter.)

The next section through the main East Devon landslips is quite strenuous. From Seaton to Lyme Regis it is about 11 kilometres of walking, but the point to remember is that once committed there is no escape route. A fold-out leaflet about the area bearing a detailed map and sketches can be bought for a few pence from Seaton Information Office on the promenade. At the eastern end of the town Seaton Bridge crosses the tidal mouth of the river Axe. Clustered here in the summer are numerous small boats; harbours and moorings are at a premium on this coast. The bridge, built in 1877, is the oldest surviving concrete bridge in England, and is beginning to show its age. Simulated masonry joints delude the casual observer into thinking it is built of stone. Having crossed the bridge, turn away from the coast and go right, up the approach road to Axe

Cliff Golf Club, then straight across the fairway into Barn Close Lane. Turn right at the coast path sign and the route leads across fields and over a stile into the National Nature Reserve. There now remain 6½ kilometres to the Dorset border – nearly 7½ as the path meanders. One kilometre beyond the boundary is Lyme Regis, the natural objective on this stretch. For the whole of that 7½ kilometres you will be passing along one or other of a number of landslips, similar in origin to Hooken landslip between Branscombe and Beer, but more wooded and laterally more extensive. Five principal slips have been recognised here. The two easterly ones, Ware and Pinhay, are probably several hundred years old, but the three westerly slips, Bindon, Dowlands and Whitlands, are early nineteenth century, and the last two in particular are well documented. They occurred over Christmas 1839.

An unusually wet autumn had allowed the rain to percolate through the overlying chalk and greensand until it met the impermeable gault clay. This had a natural dip towards the sea of about five degrees down which the upper rocks slid, breaking up the land mass into chasms,

Green woodpecker

Grasshopper warbler

isolated plateaux and short-lived offshore reefs before settling down. The movement was violent, but took several days to achieve, and for the few farm workers and their families who experienced the drama it had all the horror of an earthquake. By a strange coincidence the President of the Geological Society was staying at Lyme Regis at the time, so, naturally, the event was fully recorded.

It is estimated that about 8,000,000 tons of rock foundered, including 6 hectares of cliff-top complete with crops and hedges. Over a half-a-kilometre-long chasm some 60–120 metres wide was thus formed. The interest to naturalists is in being able to study the growth of plant and tree cover from a given point in time. The ground is so broken that it cannot be disturbed by man, so the area has become a linear nature reserve, and probably the least interfered-with bit of country along the whole of the English south coast. As the plant communities have developed, a climax of ash woodland has been reached in many parts, with a shrub layer of hazel and maple beneath. Another major habitat is scrub, and where the path passes through open areas the effect of wind pruning on the assortment of bramble, privet, hawthorn, sloe, dogwood and other species is plain to see. There are plenty of wet habitats where the dominant shrub is the sallow, and among the rocky crevices and screes the various stages of plant colonisation can be studied. Some basic grassland areas are still there, but they are being encroached upon by scrub. Lastly, there is the shoreline habitat which is not especially rich in inter-tidal seaweeds and animals, due principally to its exposure to storms, and the seepage of fresh water over the beach. This variety of habitat has encouraged many animals, birds and insects to make their homes in the area. Roe deer are the largest mammals, with badgers, foxes, rabbits and the common rodents well represented. Well over a hundred different bird species have been recorded in the landslip, including the nightingale which has nested here. I can personally vouch for the presence of adders, as I saw one at the western end coiled up on a pile of flints. It is impossible to list the vast variety of interest contained in the Reserve – fungi, mosses, ferns, butterflies, moths, and much more. The path is kept in order by Conservation Corps volunteers, but there may be stretches overdue for attention, in which case a useful ploy, providing you are wearing an anorak with a hood, is to pull the hood over your head and force a way through. For much of the way the path is out of sight and sound of the sea, so it is almost with a feeling of relief that eventually the route opens out and views ahead beckon you forward.

The end of the South Devon Coast Path comes very undramatically just after the path begins to descend through fields towards Lyme Regis, but it is the little town

Bullfinch

Eroded cliffs at Ladram Bay

On the Path, at Ladram Ba

itself which marks the end of the walk. The last descent of the walk (or the first ascent if walking east to west) is the steepest of the whole route. Tall steps, tiring to the knees after walking from Seaton (at least) lead you out into civilisation, between chalets and caravans behind the bowling green near the Cobb, Lyme's ancient harbour. From here on the path description is another story. . . .

Book list

A Book of the Seaside, Drive Publications, 1972

Nature Conservation in Devon, Devon County Council, 1977

Barrett, J H & Yonge, C M, *Pocket Guide to the Sea Shore*, Collins, 1960

Bradbeer, Grace, *The Land Changed its Face*, David & Charles, 1973. (The wartime evacuation of part of the South Hams)

Burton, S H, *The South Devon Coast*, Werner Laurie, 1954

Chope, R P (edit), *Early Tours in Devon and Cornwall*, David & Charles, 1918, reprinted 1967

Coxhead, J R W, *Old Smuggling Days in East Devon*, priv pub'd, 1954

Delderfield, Eric R, *The Raleigh Country*, Raleigh Press, 1950

Farr, Grahame, *Wreck and Rescue on the Coast of Devon*, Bradford Barton, 1968

Gill, Crispin, *Plymouth: A New History, Ice Age to the Elizabethans*, David & Charles, 1966

Hogg, Ian V, *The Coast Defences of England and Wales 1856–1956*, David & Charles, 1974

Hoskins, W G, *Devon*, Collins, 1954

Larn, Richard, *Devon Shipwrecks*, David & Charles, 1974

Minchinton, W E, *Industrial Archaeology in Devon*, Dartington Amenity Research Trust, second edition 1973

Moore, Robert, *The Birds of Devon*, David & Charles, 1969

Page, John L W, *The Coasts of Devon and Lundy Island*, Cox, 1895

Perkins, J W, *Geology Explained in South and East Devon*, David & Charles, 1971

Pevsner, Nikolaus, *The Buildings of England: South Devon*, Penguin, 1952

Pike, John R, *Portrait of Torbay*, Torbay Borough Council, n.d.

Pimlott, J A R, *The Englishman's Holiday: A Social History*, Harvester Press 1947, reprinted 1976

Pyatt, E C, *Coastal Paths of the South West*, David & Charles, 1971

Russell, Percy, *A History of Torquay and the Famous Anchorage of Torbay*, Torquay Natural History Society, 1960

Sellman, R R, *Illustrations of Devon History*, Methuen, 1962

Seymour, John, *The Companion Guide to the Coast of South-West England*, Collins, 1974

Shorter, A H, Ravenhill, W L D, Gregory, K J, *Southwest England*, Nelson, 1969

Simmons, Jack, (edit), *A Devon Anthology*, Macmillan, 1971

Smith, A, Southam J, *Good Beach Guide*, Penguin, 1973

Soper, Tony, *The Shell Book of Beachcombing*, David & Charles, 1972

Steers, J A, *The Coastline of England and Wales*, Cambridge U.P., 1969

Sutton, Anna, *A Story of Sidmouth*, priv pub'd, second edition 1959

Thomas, David St John, *A Regional History of the Railways of Great Britain Vol 1, The West Country*, David & Charles, 1966

Thompson, W Harding, *Devon: A Survey of its Coast, Moors and Rivers*, University of London Press, 1932

Vaughan, J, *The English Guide Book c1780–1870*, David & Charles, 1974

Wallace, T J, *The Axmouth-Lyme Regis Undercliffs National Nature Reserve*, Allhallows School, 1963

Willy, Margaret, *The South Hams*, Robert Hale, 1955

Various authors, *Devon Wetlands*, Devon County Council, 1977

Gazetteer

Below are a few notes about each of the larger places met with along the South Devon Coast Path. All provide accommodation and public transport, and all, except Beer, have tourist information centres – some of them seasonal.

BEER – a large fishing village. Down its main street a stream rushes in a deep channel. Hundreds of years ago the village boasted a pier for the shipment of Beer stone, but it was demolished in a storm. Honiton lace was made here (it was an East Devon cottage industry) by the womenfolk.

BRIXHAM – a characterful fishing port of local import-ance, now unashamedly a holiday resort also. Brixham fishermen were indirectly responsible for establishing Hull and Grimsby as major fishing ports on the east coast. When the Napoleonic wars ended Brixham trawlers started fishing off the Kent coast, partly to 'follow the fish' and partly to be near the London market. They then pushed on into the North Sea and claimed the discovery of the important fishing grounds there. Then, with newly-established rail links between the east coast and the

Midlands and northern markets, the development of the Humber ports was inevitable. Much of the lower part of the town abutting the harbour stands on made up ground which up to about 1800 was the old inner harbour. William, Prince of Orange, landed here on 5 November 1688 with an army of 30,000 men to save England for Protestantism. During the last war Brixham was one of the ports where the Allied Invasion Fleet embarked for the invasion of Northern Europe.

BUDLEIGH SALTERTON – Budleigh is a select watering place (the slightly old-fashioned description is intentional). It makes no claim to cater for those who like bingo and amusement arcades on holiday. The steeply shelving pebble beach deters families with small children. Millais painted his famous picture *The Boyhood of Raleigh* here. Raleigh was born 3 kilometres away inland, at Hayes Barton.

DARTMOUTH – a deep water port of great charm and atmosphere. In former times it was more important in national maritime terms than it is today, although the presence of the Britannia Royal Naval College continues the naval tradition. The Second and Third Crusade left from Dartmouth. St Saviour's Church, just above the waterfront, is well worth a visit for its 1633 west gallery and the brasses to John Hawley and his two wives. Hawley was almost certainly the 'shipman' in Chaucer's *Canterbury Tales*. Dartmouth Castle (1490) with St Petrock's Church within its walls, and Kingswear Castle (1500)

across the water, guarded the port and, if necessary, raised a chain to bar the channel in time of war.

DAWLISH – the old village of Dawlish is some distance up the valley from the beach and was a small farming community. Development to link the village with the beach went on throughout the last century, when the stream was landscaped and the gardens laid out. Jane Austen knew Dawlish, as did Dickens: Nicholas Nickleby was 'born' here. A stroll up the stream – the Dawlish water – is a pleasant diversion. There are black swans, and foot-long trout can be seen swimming unconcernedly beneath the ducks.

EXMOUTH – became popular with the gentry during the Napoleonic wars when people couldn't travel to the continent. Lady Nelson and Lady Byron lived for a time on the Beacon, the attractive elevated terrace of Georgian houses overlooking the sea front. Because of its long, sandy beach it later developed as a family resort, and as such it has remained. Recent excavations (1977) on the site of a new shopping development have revealed the foundations of buildings dating from the fourteenth and fifteenth centuries. The town's growth has been poorly documented so this discovery has proved a settlement at Exmouth well before written reference.

PAIGNTON – the original settlement was some distance inland, but development reached out towards the railway from 1859, and by 1901 the population had trebled, and is still growing. Paignton became the family resort of Torbay, being flatter than Torquay, and possessing more accessible beaches. It now has an excellent shopping centre.

PLYMOUTH – it is fitting that the trek along the South Devon Coast Path should start from Plymouth, as many other journeys – usually by sea – have begun from here. Tall ships races, single-handed craft races, the *Mayflower*, Drake and his fleet against the Armada – all these events, and many more, have begun on the spacious waters of Plymouth Sound, surely, after the River Thames in London, the most evocative stretch of water in Great Britain. The city of Plymouth was almost destroyed by bombing in the last war, but it has been rebuilt to a new plan of vistas and boulevards based on the Hoe, that nationally-loved promenade with its monuments and memories. Around the corner to the west, up the Hamoaze, is the dockyard, still important despite the reduction in British numerical naval strength.

SALCOMBE – a very attractive little town – Devon's farthest south – now almost entirely devoted to the summer boating trade. The navy blue of the yachting fraternity seems to fill the narrow streets, making the booted coast-path walker feel very out of place. Fort Charles, off North Sands beach, withstood a siege during the Civil War.

SEATON – a curious seaside resort, having at its western end something of the placid atmosphere of Budleigh Salterton, but changing as one proceeds to the eastern end of the town, where there is a large holiday camp. The 2½ kilometres of disused railway track from the site of Seaton station to Colyford have been turned into a tramway along which a double-decker tram runs during the summer.

SIDMOUTH – is a quite exceptional seaside town because of its architectural attractiveness. In the area there are 484 buildings or groups of buildings listed as of special architectural and historic interest. Many of them were built by 'people of quality' in the years before and immediately after 1800, and have the light touch of the Regency period. The trees planted in the large gardens have matured, giving the town a mellow prospect. A good place for shopping.

TEIGNMOUTH – all one expects of a seaside resort – sand, pier, boats, promenade, seafront recreation area, and shops to look at when it's too cold to sit on the beach. Tucked away behind the town centre are narrow winding streets with some interesting pubs. The town was badly hit during the last war by German aircraft. The harbour is usually busy despatching ball clay to European destinations. Shaldon, across the estuary, is a pleasant village of harmonious nineteenth century cottages.

TORQUAY – it seems incredible that the largest Devon seaside resort should have been but a small fishing village with a population of less than 1,000 in 1800. Much of the story of its growth is contained in the chapter on the rise of the Devon holiday industry. The native limestone everywhere asserts itself, especially along the route through the town, which also passes near the shops.

Useful addresses

Devon Tourism Office
County Estate Surveyor's Department
County Hall
Exeter
Exeter 55794

West Country Tourist Board
Trinity Court
37 Southernhay East
Exeter
Exeter 76351

Western National Bus Co
National House
Queen Street
Exeter
Exeter 74191/4

The Ramblers' Association
1-5 Wandsworth Road
London SW8 2LJ
01-582 6878

Youth Hostels Association (England and Wales)
Trevelyan House
8 St Stephen's Hill
St Albans
Herts AL1 2DY
St Albans 55215

South West Way Association
Assistant Secretary:
Mrs D Y Lancey
'Kynance'
15 Old Newton Road
Kingskerswell
Newton Abbot
Devon

The South West Way Association was formed in 1973 to promote the interests of users of the South-West Peninsula Coast Path. For an annual subscription of £1·50 members receive three *Newsletters* a year and a free copy of each new footpath description as it is issued. These are write-ups for short sections of the path. The SWWA also publishes a guide each spring which gives up-to-date information on ferries, accommodation, and many other useful facts.

Ferries and river crossings

Periods of operation and timetables may change from year to year, so it is essential to get up-to-date information before setting out. The details below reflect the 1980 schedule.

Warren Point to Noss Mayo (River Yealm)

Len Carter & Son
Riverslea
Yealm Road
Newton Ferrers
Plymouth

Newton Ferrers 872210 and 872481
May to mid-July daily: 0900 to 1700 as required
Mid-July to September daily: 0900 to 1800 as required

The ferry is often stationed at the third point of this triangular crossing, below the Yealm Hotel, so you are advised to shout or wave to attract attention. A telephone call in advance is recommended.

Mothecombe to Wonwell (River Erme)

No ferry

The river can usually be waded one hour each side of low water on the line of the old ford from the county road east of Mothecombe to Wonwell beach from slipway to slipway. Floodwater coming downriver, or heavy seas coming into the estuary can make this a hazardous operation. Times of

Stoke

high tide are given daily in *The Western Morning News*, and low tides can be worked out in advance from a nautical almanac. There is no right of way along the river bank and there is no other way across the estuary except for the road detour of 13 or so kilometres via Sequers Bridge on the A379.

Bigbury (Cockleridge) to Bantham (River Avon)

Mr H Cater
Yorick
West Buckland
Thurlestone
Kingsbridge

Thurlestone 593

End of May to September, also two weeks at Easter:
Monday to Saturday 1000 to 1100
1500 to 1600
also on Sundays in July and August

It is possible to wade the river when the ferry is not running, provided the weather is not rough and the river in flood, but you may be up to your thighs in water. The river is forded below the ferry crossing from a hedge with pine trees on the west bank towards a castellated building on the east bank. The attempt should not be made anywhere else because of deep water, soft sand and tidal ebbs.

Salcombe to East Portlemouth (Salcombe harbour)

Limhart Limited
8 Currer Street
Bradford, W. Yorks

Bradford 28375 (or Salcombe 2061 – boat house only)

Operates daily all the year:
Summer Monday to Saturday 0700 to 2050
Sundays   0800 to 1950

Winter Monday to Saturday 0700 to 1950
Sundays   0800 to 1850

Wonwell

Dartmouth (Lower Ferry) to Kingswear (River Dart)

Dart Pleasure Craft Limited
5 Lower Street
Dartmouth
Dartmouth 3144

April to October: Monday to Saturday 0700–2300
                             Sunday 0800–2300
October to April: Monday to Saturday only 0730–1830

Shaldon (beach) to Teignmouth (harbour beach) (River Teign)

Teignbridge District Council
Channel View
Teignmouth

Teignmouth 6271

October to March: Monday to Friday only 0800–1700
March to October: daily   0800–1700   then   progressively
                      later to 2200 in high season

Starcross to Exmouth (River Exe)

Devon Dock, Pier and Steamship Co Ltd
Dock Office
Exmouth

Exmouth 72009

May to September:
Monday to Friday   8 sailings daily   ⎫ to connect with
Saturdays   6 sailings   ⎬ trains from
Sundays   5 sailings   ⎭ Starcross station
Check exact dates and times

The Country Code

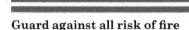

Guard against all risk of fire

Every year costly damage is done by fire to crops, plantations, woodlands and heaths. Picnic fires not properly put out are one cause. A cigarette thrown away or a pipe carelessly knocked out can start a raging inferno. Be careful – a spark may do terrible damage and destroy a lifetime's work.

Fasten all gates

Animals, if they stray, can do great damage to crops and to themselves too. Wandering animals are a menace to themselves and to others on country roads. Even if you find a gate open, always shut it after you.

Keep dogs under proper control

It is natural for a dog to chase anything that will run. Keep yours out of temptation's way. Animals are easily frightened. The chasing of a ewe or cow may mean the loss of valuable young. Town-bred dogs run great risks from traffic in narrow roads. When near animals or walking along the road, keep your dog on the lead, if it cannot be kept under close control.

Keep to the paths across farm land

Crops are damaged by treading at any stage of growth. Patches of flattened corn in a field make it difficult to harvest. Grass also is a valuable crop, remember. So please walk in single file on field paths. This keeps the track well defined and saves the crop on either side.

Avoid damaging fences, hedges and walls

If you force your way through a fence or hedge, you will weaken it. Where a man has gone an animal may follow. Stones from walls rolled down slopes may injure people and animals, destroy fences, and damage crops or machines. Use gates and stiles.

Leave no litter

All litter is unsightly. Broken glass, tins and plastic bags are dangerous; they very easily maim livestock. Tins, bottles and stones in fields damage costly machinery. This may hold up work which it is vital to finish while the weather lasts. So take your picnic remains and other litter home with you.

Safeguard water supplies

Water is precious in the country. Never wash dishes or bathe in somebody's water supply or foul it in any other way, or interfere with water-troughs set for cattle.

Protect wild life, wild plants and trees

Wild flowers give more pleasure to more people if left to grow. Plants should never be uprooted. Trees are valuable as well as beautiful: if they are damaged their health and beauty is harmed. Birds and their eggs, animals, plants and trees should be left alone.

Go carefully on country roads

Country roads have special dangers. Blind corners, hump-backed bridges, slow-moving farm machinery and led or driven animals are all hazards for the motorist. Walk carefully, too. It is generally safer to walk on the right, facing oncoming traffic.

Respect the life of the countryside

The life of the country centres on its work. While you are there, try to fit in. The countryman has to leave his belongings in the open, roads and paths run through his place of business, and the public are on trust. His work often involves hard labour. He has to keep early hours. So make as little noise as possible when you pass through his village in the evening. Be considerate, leave things alone, and so repay the local people for the pleasure their countryside has given you.

Slapton S
in Start B